Dolores,
LIKE THE RIVER

LAURA L. PADGETT

Illustrations by Sally M. Cordrey

WESTBOW
PRESS
A DIVISION OF THOMAS NELSON

All Scripture quotations, unless otherwise indicated, are taken from the Holy Bible, New International Version, NIV, Copyright 1973, 1978, and 1984 by International Bible Society.

Illustrations by Sally M. Cordrey (sally.cordrey@gmail.com) used with permission.

Cover photo of Dolores River near Dolores, Colorado, by Laura L. Padgett.

Photo of Laura at the Dolores River by Keith Padgett.

Lyrics of "Days of Elijah" by Robin Mark, © 1996 Daybreak Music, Ltd, used by permission.

Author bio photo by Life Touch Photos, used with permission.

WestBow Press books may be ordered through booksellers or by contacting:

WestBow Press
A Division of Thomas Nelson
1663 Liberty Drive
Bloomington, IN 47403
www.westbowpress.com
1 (866) 928-1240

ISBN: 978-1-4908-1438-4 (sc)
ISBN: 978-1-4908-1437-7 (hc)
ISBN: 978-1-4908-1439-1 (e)

Library of Congress Control Number: 2013919647

Printed in the United States of America.

WestBow Press rev. date: 12/10/2013

Contents

To the Ocean

This work is dedicated to my husband, Keith; my son, Gabriel; and my sister, Mary. They are my three best friends forever. And to the memory of the woman who taught me how to appreciate my family and friends: Dolores.

Acknowledgments

When we discover a passion for an art, it is our duty to share that passion and art with others. When we choose to share our art for the Lord, out of gratitude for His great gifts, the product of that sharing becomes ministry. No one does ministry alone. There are many people who supported this work, yet it is not possible to mention everyone by name. I would, however, like to publically thank some of my biggest supporters who traveled with me along this path, in order to bring Dolores's and my story to print.

My husband, Keith, has been chief keeper of my dreams, monitor of distractions, wiper of my tears, up lifter, encourager, cheerleader, maker of many late-night meals, and tireless confidence builder when I could do nothing but doubt myself, my abilities, and the purpose of my endeavors.

Dorothy Cramer is a thorough and spot-on editor whose advice was tempered by a gentle spirit that always sought to speak truth in love. Because of her work, I am proud to present this book to the Lord and to those who may find it worth the read.

Sally Cordrey is an extraordinarily gifted artist who designed illustrations with little to work from but my vague visions. Additionally, she is a faithful and patient friend.

Lisa Alejandre, Sally Cordrey, Dorothy Cramer, Michelle Farrell, and Carolyn English are among my closest lady friends. They have encouraged and endorsed me as I periodically defined, refined, and redefined myself.

My brothers and sisters at Regis University and North Highland Presbyterian Church in Denver, as well as Faith Lutheran Church in Golden, have been rich resources for clarity. I particularly want to thank the God Chicks Bible Study group at FLC and the Ladies Bible Study/ knitting group, along with Pastor Carol and Pastor Ashley at NHPC for teaching me it is okay to show and tell "just like it is."

My exercise buddies in Coach Stacy's fitness class motivated me weekly by sharing their excitement about the release of this book.

The dance teams I have moved with over the years, including St. Brendan's School of Irish Dance, Miss Gwen Bowen's Dance Studio, and Destination Dance, have taught me how to love the dance. The dance ministry teams of Grace and Glory, Quickened Ministries, The King's Table 2013, The Rocky Mountain Sacred Dance Guild, and The Steps of Faith Ladies Dance Team have taught me how to offer all my gifts, including dance and writing, to God as I praise and worship Him with my whole being.

To all of you, I say, "Thank you for believing in and supporting me. I love you and praise God for you every day."

A Note from the Author

In some cases throughout this narrative, characters are presented precisely as they appeared in my life. In other cases, I have employed artistic privilege in the form of combining two or more people and/or changing names. When calling upon characters to reinforce the storyline, I have introduced them only through their relationship to my growth and my story. In all but one or two cases, characters have been shown in a positive light. If readers find a similarity between themselves, or someone they know, and a character within these pages, it would be unwise to assume or assign absolute identities. It was never my intention to tell the stories of anyone but Dolores and me. History is told from the lens of the storyteller, and each of us would relate history differently.

The events chronicled within these pages are, with few exceptions, recorded chronologically. But in some instances, I chose to combine or rearrange events into more efficient timelines, in an effort to spare a tedious literary journey.

Introduction

When I was twenty-five years old, I moved from Denver to a town in western Colorado called Montrose. I supposed that, like many my age, I was "finding myself" by running from home. In reality, the motivation for my move was a belief that I could find the internal peace I craved by manipulating my life's external elements.

While in Montrose, I found a relationship with God through the Lord Jesus Christ. I began a personal faith journey that challenged and eventually dismissed my belief that if there was a God, the chances were slim He would ever find a place in my world or I in His. On my spiritual voyage, I came to understand that I was loved for just who I am. I learned that God wanted a relationship with me. Coming from a family destroyed by alcoholism and abuse, this was not a message imprinted on my sense of self.

The Bible tells us that God loves and accepts us unconditionally. I soon found He does not just talk a good game. He supplies people, here on earth, who live and give His kind of love. He brought a woman named Dolores into my life. Over the next thirty-five years, she extended that unconditional love along with unwavering patience and understanding as I struggled to find my spiritual feet. She endlessly supplied wise instruction for growth in the Lord and provided an example of unflappable integrity. We met when she was sixty-five and I was twenty-six. It was through Dolores that God taught me about self-acceptance, forgiveness, dealing with loss, exposing the lies I believed about myself and others, living in joy, finding my gifts, and using them for His glory.

We were two completely different women, Dolores and I. Our age difference of forty years was only one area of dissimilarity. Dolores had had a privileged upbringing and education. I was a kid with little education beyond high school, and I'd been raised by parents who barely scraped by financially and spent most of their extra time and energy on drinking and fighting. She was soft-spoken, even-tempered, and refined in manners. I was a rough and tough, beer-swilling, cigarette-smoking, hard-playing, hotheaded young woman who was more at home in a biker bar than a sitting room. She was a staunch conservative with 1940s values. I represented the liberal girls from the 1970s, with values dependent upon my whims and perceived needs at any given time. Dolores was a woman of faith matured through a lifetime. I had more than a small challenge in trusting a stranger on a cross for something I really didn't believe in: eternal salvation.

From a human lens, this relationship would be considered unlikely to form let alone last for well over a quarter of a century. It had to be ordained by heaven. This was a master plan by the master planner to teach me about love—the one element that above all will sustain us through time, age, and life's various predicaments.

It is my prayer that as you follow this story, you will (if you don't now) appreciate the Master and His great plans, as well as the teachers and mentors He sends to bring those glorious plans to fruition in your life. And when your turn comes to assume the role of teacher/mentor, I pray you will be willing to flow as a quenching, healing, and nurturing river in the life of another.

The Small Droplet

A river can start as a small drop of water landing on parched soil. If the land will yield to the tiny drop, it is possible to receive relief from an almost fatal state of dryness. It is the droplet's willingness to be used, and the land's willingness to relinquish its stance of non-yielding, that can bring new life to both.

It is a small start, but it is a beginning all the same.

CHAPTER 1

On the Run

"Are you out of your mind?" Lana, one of my friends and coworkers, sat in disbelief. While we were having beers, one night after work, I announced I was moving from Denver. My plan was to relocate to Montrose, a small town in the middle of a valley and farmland on the western side of the Continental Divide in Colorado.

She fired question after question. "What can possibly interest you in some little mountain town? What life can that place offer someone who is used to living in a city with limitless artistic, educational, and cultural benefits? And how do you plan to make a living?"

"Look, I have already explained this," I replied patiently. "I need to get away from here, and I need a change, period. I have a job waiting for me there."

Frankly, I was getting weary of well-meaning people demanding explanations from me. I was over twenty-five years old. I didn't owe anyone anything. I made it this far without anyone's help, and I was fully competent to continue on with my life. The interference, with unsolicited advice, was becoming intolerable.

"How will you move? How will you take your stuff over there?" She wanted to know some of the details. I found that encouraging.

"Well, that's where I am hoping for some help from my friends," I admitted. I was grateful Lana was moving away from inquiring about my motives and my sanity. The new conversational direction gave me opportunity to ask for her assistance. I was counting on the fact that Lana rarely resisted opportunities to participate in novel exploits.

I lit a cigarette and continued unfolding my plans. "I'm selling some belongings. The place I'm renting is fully furnished. My old Chevy will carry some of my worldly goods. Since you have a large van, I am asking you to transport the other things I plan to keep. I'll pay for gas and food."

"Okay," she said, "but why Montrose? What is over there that interests you? Laura, I'm going to miss you. Are you sure about this? I mean you just started back to school and are dating a really cool guy. What about all that?"

"I don't think that relationship is what I really want; and as I keep saying, I need to get away from here and away from my mother. I've put up with her last hurtful stunt. I don't care if she is a drunk. That is her choice, and drinking has always been more important to her than her family. I just need to find my own life without worrying about bailing her out of jail or plucking her off the streets. I'm tired of the vomit, the drunken friends, and the midnight calls to rescue her. I've seen all the dumps on Larimer Street that I care to in this lifetime, thank you." I stubbed out one cigarette and lit another.

After a few minutes of silence, I stopped trying to persuade her. "Look, if helping me is a problem for you, forget it. I'll get there with what I can carry in my car," I said. I tried to make my voice reflect the resolve in my heart and gut. No one was going to stop this move.

"All right, I'll help you. But you still haven't answered my question. How did you decide on Montrose?" she asked.

I told her I answered an advertisement in a trade magazine for employment. When I went to the job interview, the town looked like a perfect place for what I hoped would be a new start. It was small, quaint, in the middle of beautiful country, and 250 miles from my current home and my mother. Lana shrugged and again assured me she would assist with my move.

I was relieved. Moving was one thing, but leaving all of my worldly belongings behind was something altogether different. For a moment, as I talked this through with her, I felt sadness for leaving my life in Denver, especially because my two sisters lived there. I couldn't think about that now. I had to go. I had to.

On the Saturday of my departure, several people, including my sisters, were there to help with the final loading. No one seemed to share my enthusiasm for my newly chosen direction. I put their feelings and objections aside. I was leaving, period. They could come and visit any time they wanted, or not.

The trip from Denver to Montrose took about five hours. I drove a 1950 Chevy sedan I had won in a bet when the Pittsburgh Steelers beat the Dallas Cowboys in the 1976 Super Bowl. My jalopy was loaded with records, stuffed toys, clothes, a few plants, and several cartons of Marlboros. The rest of my worldly goods preceded me out of town, in the van.

I was born and raised in Denver, but my family spent little to no time playing in the nearby mountains. My father had a heart condition that made it difficult to breathe in higher altitudes. Denver's elevation, at one mile above sea level, was about all he could take in the years before his death at age fifty-six. My mother usually complained of motion sickness and didn't like traveling on the winding roads over mountain passes. For me, the mountain scenery was no more recognizable than it would have been to a first-time Colorado visitor.

There were, however, some familiar spots along the journey out of town. A memory of one picnic near the small town of Bailey, off Highway 285, came to mind. I remembered Papa coming to get me out of a tree when I climbed too high and cried for rescue. He laughed and teased me but had no problem responding to the pleas of his middle child. There were times my dad could be very tender and gentle. But I was hard-pressed to find a lot of those warm, fuzzy memories.

I thought there were probably *some* good things about being in a family but, personally, I had developed a preference for flying solo. Refusing to be melancholy about leaving Denver behind, I focused on the September landscape.

In the fall, Colorado high country is fantastic. The aspen trees dance on the breeze as they shamelessly swirl their multicolored frocks. Little creeks appear from time to time along the winding roads and add voices to nature's concert, in support of the trees' choreography. Copious amounts of green, gold, and brown wild grasses rustle in response to grazing by small and large creatures.

We made our way over Kenosha Pass and descended onto a long stretch of road running through Park County. The area is called South Park. This particular piece of land, for the most part, is flat and supports ranches. A keen eye can pick up the graceful form of an antelope sharing feeding ground with cattle and sheep. Fields are populated with an array of fall wild flowers. All this open space rests in the shadows of the rugged Rocky Mountains. Towering, treeless peaks sport snowcaps that serve as headgear year-round.

The beauty caused my breath to catch in my throat. The doubts that incessantly played as background music in my mind were momentarily silenced. Truly, this was a good decision. This was the right decision.

Lana and I stopped to stretch our legs about halfway through the park. "This is like a completely different world. This is where you are going to live, Laura. Maybe this isn't such a stupid idea after all. It's beautiful," she announced.

"Yeah, thanks. I know. But this isn't exactly my destination. That's over a pass or two yet," I informed her.

She didn't hear me. She was busy snapping pictures in every direction. I pulled out a cigarette, lit it, blew out the match, and put the spent fire implement in my jacket pocket. My father had always said that careless humans were usually responsible for forest and wild grass fires. On the rare occasions when I found myself out of doors, my father's words served to keep me in proper ecological posture.

A different world was right. I hadn't seen so much open land in a very long time. The smell of the fields, and the sight of the looming mountains, provided a calming balm over my hesitant heart that waxed and waned between righteous certainty of my new direction and viewing each passing mile in the light of loss. I missed my sisters already. I felt guilty about leaving my mother without telling her what was going on, or even calling to say good-bye. I took a long drag on my cigarette.

"She is not my responsibility. She chose her life. Let her live it. I am going to live mine," I said out loud to the silent mountain range bordering the park.

After we made our way through South Park, we climbed, crossed, and descended Monarch Pass. The forested areas held my attention and provided return to the positive swing of the pendulum of uncertainty. There was cleanliness about these surroundings. The aged pine trees exuded a strength that testified to their resilience and determination in the face of the severe Colorado winters. Looking at the rugged greenery, I felt an identity with the determination it takes to survive harsh circumstances.

Arriving in Montrose evoked utterings of delight from my traveling companion. "Wow, this place is gorgeous. Can you just imagine all the pictures you can take? And look, there's a restaurant and everything," Lana observed.

"Good," I snarled. "I need a beer. I hope this place isn't dry."

The five-hour drive from Denver to Montrose was accompanied only by soft drinks as liquid sustenance. Drinking and driving terrified me. The memories never seemed to fade of the accidents and DUIs my mother had racked up, not to mention expenses for bailing her out of jail. Then there were the court appearances. But that was all behind me now. She could bail herself out, appear before judges solo, and deal with her own accidents and the financial disasters resulting from her choices. I was free—free from her and free from my past. She couldn't hurt me now.

Lana and I ate, drank, and then found the little apartment I was renting. After unloading my car, we took off in the old Chevy to explore the town. To our delight, there were several bars and dancing establishments.

"This will do nicely," I said. "This will do nicely, indeed."

The next morning, Lana headed home, but not before I treated her to breakfast at one of the local greasy spoons. During breakfast, she said it seemed like I already knew my way around and was going to do just fine.

I let her leave without telling her that I, in fact, had been to Montrose while in high school for a sporting event. She didn't need to know that my parents were from Grand Junction, just an hour north, and that on trips to the Junction my family had driven through this little spot many times. It wasn't important to inform her that this was a frequent trip for my father and his three daughters when he needed to deposit us for a few weeks, with family, while he searched for our wayward mother. Although Montrose was to be my new home, returning to Grand Junction with its memories of fear and abandonment did *not* factor into my plans.

After breakfast, I watched my friend drive toward the highway leading back to Denver. I tried to silence the sad, little voice protesting that the last contact to my old life was heading back to the Mile High City without me. The seesaw of feelings, with positive affirmation on one side and guilt with trepidation on the other, was getting old. I swallowed hard and reminded myself I was finally free. That was the biggest positive imaginable in my book.

After waving to Lana's rearview mirror, I lit a cigarette, popped the top on a fresh beer, and walked into my new life.

CHAPTER 2

Not Exactly What I Signed Up For

By my light, it didn't take much to please me. As long as I could find good food, good drink, reasonable working hours, a place to dance, and a shoe store capable of keeping up with an insatiable appetite for footwear, I could live just about any place.

There were, however, some things I hadn't factored into what I thought was a flawless scheme of escape. I missed my sisters desperately. I considered them my closest friends. I can't say I trusted the sisters with everything in my life, but I confided in them more than anyone else in my world. They missed me too. That affected me in a way I hadn't seen coming. I felt sad and guilty.

It was not in my nature to backpedal an issue. My philosophy went something like this: When one is surviving on wits and guts, there is no room for second-guessing personal decisions. No one is allowed a do-over of the past. Spending time retro-gazing always diverts attention from the present, and the future. This logical philosophy, born out of self-sufficiency, kept me from drowning in the river of regrets on most days.

Another knot in my perfectly tapestried new life was the cost of living. The wages were much lower in Montrose than in Denver. I had counted on that. What I hadn't counted on was the daily cost of survival being higher. Everything, from toilet paper to pork chops, cost more than I was used to paying in Denver. This put a dent in the "fun" side of budgetary expenses. To make up for this, I volunteered for extra shifts. This, of course, affected allotted time for a social life. At this juncture, it appeared little was going according to script.

I made few friends, and along with my "kiss my cookies" attitude, difficulties on the job surfaced and multiplied at an alarming rate. I isolated myself, ate alone, and invented excuses to avoid taking coffee breaks with other employees. I had several run-ins with my supervisor, which made working conditions close to intolerable.

My field was female dominated and, without exception, I preferred the company of men to women. My mother had proven to be unreliable, to say the least. By my lens, this left women in the category of untrustworthy. With the exception of a high school girlfriend or two, the majority of my companions in Denver were men. So it was no surprise that the one person I found myself drawn to, in a purely platonic way, was male. Eventually, we began to take coffee breaks together and work on some of the same projects.

He was in his late twenties, had been married and divorced, and had one young child. His name was Eric. He did not seem to be interested in anything but friendship. That suited me down to the ground. This proved to be a satisfactory friendship, except for one thing. He was a religious person.

Oh brother. One of those, I thought.

I had, in my teen and early-adult years, avoided getting sucked into any kind of a God culture. I tried to be tolerant of people with views that differed from mine. But more times than not, my patience wore thin. I became bored and did little to hide my feelings. I had become downright hostile on several occasions when people went to preaching at me or prying into my personal thoughts on where I was going to spend eternity. I didn't believe in any of that stuff, and I had no interest in altering my belief system. I couldn't even fake an interest in living a life that looked dull beyond all reasonable tolerance and was based on some ancient book of rules.

Okay, I thought, *I like this guy, and he is turning out to be a good friend in all other ways. So I guess I can put up with his Jesus talk once in a while. What can it hurt?*

My skeptical mind, ever the analyzer and on high alert around the clock, took stock of the situation by weighing all the facts. He had a lot of things going for him. He was nice, didn't force his views down my throat, and had some interesting stuff to say about other things besides church. He wasn't interested in me as anything more than a friend. But the biggest thing going for him was his gender. He was not female.

Although I can't say my new friend sang the song of the zealot or evangelist, he did manage to infuse our conversations with his Christian values from time to time. On those occasions, I practiced patience and feigned interest by nodding my head and smiling with lips only. Then I usually began mentally composing my grocery list.

This was easy enough and worked for a few months. However, one small problem arose. There was another person at work, Len, who also had this Jesus thing going on. When Eric and Len started talking churchy stuff, I usually found a way to politely exit the room before I lost my temper and told them what nonsense I thought it all was.

I reasoned that this just wasn't "my thing." I told myself that I had made it this far after my father died, when I was a teenager, leaving me to be raised by a mother who stayed drunk and unemployed. Finding myself homeless and paying off my mother's debt, as well as keeping her from sleeping courtesy of Denver County, did little to encourage me to embrace the loving heavenly father that Eric and Len talked about.

This same heavenly father apparently frowned on anyone going out on weekends and drinking and dancing until all hours of the night. I came to this conclusion because that was one thing Eric simply was not interested in doing. It never occurred to me that he had his small child on the weekends. I felt his reluctance to party was his only real character flaw. If I wanted to partake in such activities, it was up to me to find some folks who also enjoyed my brand of extracurriculars.

The search didn't take long. I hooked up with some people working in the same organization who also liked to trip the life fandango. I met one woman, who was younger than me by about five years, in the lunchroom. After running into her and her roommate around town a few times, we began to hang around on a regular basis, frequenting the local bars and dancing.

The nature of my work required a clear mind, so I chose not to party during the week. This worked out well because I never had to explain a hangover, late arrivals, or why I smelled like a brewery to my friend who preferred Jesus to bright lights, cold beer, and rock and roll. It actually was country music, but I could dance to it. That was all I cared about.

I hadn't been prepared for how hard it was to live a dual life. However, I managed minimal slip-ups and only an occasional reference to a wild night down at one of the local watering holes. It was during one of the slip-up times that a serious rent in my relationship with Eric materialized.

One of the gals I had been frequenting the bars with popped her head into the break room when Eric and I were having coffee. She asked if I'd managed to make it home on Friday night after winning the "chug fest." Upon confirming my safe arrival, I smiled at Eric. He quickly looked away from me. An odd feeling in my stomach and a flush to my cheeks put me into a defensive mental posture. I excused myself and made a speedy departure.

Maybe it was being busted in my dualism. Perhaps I was angry with myself for feeling embarrassed and like I had to explain to, or ask permission from, anyone. But I felt as if I had disappointed Eric, and I was ashamed of myself.

In my best attempt at justifying my unfamiliar feelings, I began to make a case against this man, who I felt was seeing me in a light he didn't like, passing a judgment and even a sentence on me. In my eyes, this really was too much to put up with. Hadn't I listened to him go on and on for months about church picnics, Sunday school, and something called the gospel? Hadn't I extended patience when Len joined in on the chorus of, "Life is just ducky with Jesus?" Hadn't I been polite when my friend rejected my attempts at getting him to come along for a night of real fun instead of sticking his head in some ancient and irrelevant book that he carried with him like a sack lunch? Well, hadn't I?

Before I knew what was happening, I mentally passed through the garden gate and marched right up the steps to the door of the house called "Righteous Indignation" at the corner of "I Don't Need Anybody Avenue" and "How Dare You Street." I imagined my abrupt departure may have hurt, and even shocked, my friend. I told myself I didn't care. But I did care. Still, I reasoned, I had a right to live any way I wanted. I decided I didn't need him or his God.

When the workday was finished, I clocked out and made my way, on foot, to my little house. The exercise proved to be a satisfactory way to stomp off some of my irritation. I ran up the front porch steps, went in the door, and marched straight to the refrigerator. After popping the top from a beer, I took a large gulp of the cold tonic and a lit a cigarette.

Then I spent the rest of the evening fuming at my friend for his audacity.

CHAPTER 3

Nowhere to Hide

The only good thing about the coolness between Eric and me was the fact that I didn't have to spend energy trying to be someone besides me. There was relief from that, and I soon slipped into a life with friends who had more in common with me. We spent time in the bars or in each other's homes drinking, making dinners, and listening to music. Sometimes, we took trips to the Black Canyon, the Olathe Bluegrass Festival, or the warm waters of the Ouray Hot Springs.

All of these spots, and more, surrounding Montrose provided ample opportunity for partying and eating. My friends and I enjoyed four-wheeling adventures, in open-topped Jeeps, through the switchback roads of the glorious San Juan Mountains. The last activity was new to me and offered an education in the wilderness to this refugee from the Mile High City. As long as I had a drink or two and some smokes, I complied with the wishes of others and offered little resistance to the attempts at turning this city kid into a country girl.

Although I didn't grow tired of the parties and friends, I also enjoyed sitting on my front porch, sipping a cold beer, and basking in the quiet aloneness. This proved to be a satisfactory way to spend time as long as the melancholies didn't set in over missing my sisters, not being able to make ends meet, or being too broke to buy as many shoes as I felt I needed.

It was during one of these highly reflective sessions one night when a man came up to my porch and asked me a question. I don't remember the question. But I do remember he sat down on the steps, uninvited, and just made small talk.

Where I grew up, strangers were not initially trusted. His sudden appearance made me a little nervous. I watched him carefully and noticed he had the hands of a person who had spent some time in hard labor. I summed him up as a probable ex-con who was preying on lone females. His fingers were short and thick. There were pronounced knobs on his knuckles. He caught me staring at his hands, stood up, put them in his pockets, and said he had to go to work.

I asked the stranger where he worked. He told me he was a cook at a local restaurant and bar on Main Street. He was waiting for a job in construction to open up. That was what he really enjoyed and what he felt he was good at. That explained his knobby knuckles and made me feel a little easier about the past I had imagined he carried with him.

He gave his name as Bob and said he enjoyed meeting me. I thought about telling him I was Debbie, Linda, or something other than Laura, but I changed my mind. I offered no name and didn't protest when he announced his departure. He said he might stop by some other time, and then walked away. I neither confirmed an invitation nor denied him one. He seemed like an interesting guy. He was a little scary, maybe, but interesting.

During the next several months, I had many evening visits from Bob. He said he lived a few doors down the street, in a little blue house on the north side. We talked about sports, cars, Montrose, and our jobs. It was not a romantic relationship; that was an understanding we both had without verbalizing it. I found this strange because I had, so far, met two attractive and interesting men but really had no desire to pursue anything beyond friendship with them. Prior to my move to Montrose, it had been my habit to never be without a boyfriend, or sometimes two at one time. I liked men. I felt whole when I was someone's girl and somewhat less than whole when I wasn't. I wondered if I was losing interest in romance.

Bob only popped in around the early evening hours and never stayed more than an hour or two because of his work schedule. I figured that if he worked in a bar/restaurant, he probably wasn't going to judge me for drinking beer and enjoying the party life.

That was one thing that made me very comfortable in his presence. He accepted me just as I was. There were other things too, but I couldn't put my finger on any of them. I just knew I was always glad to see him. And I was relieved that he wanted nothing more, from me, than my company. I also knew he wasn't female, which meant there was a good chance he could be trusted. I trusted him enough to tell him about my life, where I'd come from, and what I was running from.

One evening during a conversation about what I wanted from my life and how I saw my future shaping up, I noticed how calm and contented Bob seemed. I liked that. More than *liked*, I admired that. I wanted that. I wanted that.

I knew very little of any substance about Bob, so I decided to ask him about his life. He said he just traveled around the country, landing mostly in small towns. He liked small towns because in them it was easier for him to find contentment in God's creation.

Oh no, I thought. *Oh no, please.*

I ventured forward with another question, but I already knew how this was going to turn out. "Find contentment in God's creation?" I asked.

"Yes," he said. "Everywhere you look and everywhere you go, you will see His handiwork. He did all of this just for us. He loves us and knows us better than we know ourselves."

"Loves us, huh?" I could feel my temper dial quickly revolving to the out-of-control setting.

"He loves us so much He sent His Son, Jesus, to die for us and give us new and eternal life." He stopped talking when he saw my face.

I don't know if it has ever been documented that a person can actually feel their features turn monster-like. But my face burned, as if I'd been too long in the hot sun. I feared my eyeballs would pop from my head if they didn't in fact melt from the heat rising around them. Without realizing it, I was screaming at the top of my lungs.

"Oh yeah? Died for us, huh? Why? What for? Does your God love us so much that He would subject three innocent little girls to a life with a mother who didn't want them and constantly abandoned them to alcohol? Does your God want us so much that He sends His representatives on earth to refuse children, little children, admittance to His big, glorious churches because their father was not in good standing? Does your God think so highly of us that He kills the only parent a child knows and leaves her in her teens, virtually on her own, in a world that only wants to harm her?" I decided to give him a chance to respond and then changed my mind. I continued my rant-a-thon.

"How does your God, your Jesus or whoever He is, find it in His plan to leave little children in an unsafe place while they witness horrors of domestic violence and disgusting drunken behaviors? Where is your God when a little girl cries out at night for the screaming and hitting and bleeding to stop? Does He even care? Does He understand the hurt? I have made my own way in this world with little guidance from a loving presence of any kind. I don't need your loving God."

With pauses only for lighting another cigarette and opening another beer, the tirade went on. Bob sat motionless. There was no terror in his eyes and no shrinking from the rage-fueled story of a young woman who blamed this God, this Jesus, for not stepping in, for not stepping up.

When the anger was spent, I turned my back to him and asked him to leave and never come back. "You are just like all the rest: untrustworthy, unreliable, trying to remake me. I will never be good enough, and I can never forget the brutality that has been my life. Your God has no understanding of my pain or of anyone's pain for that matter. He knows nothing about rejection, confusion, and humiliation. He knows nothing." The last word was uttered in a whisper.

Adopting a softer tone that reflected my exhaustion, I said, "Bob, I've heard all of this before. I've heard that this Jesus can change a life and offer hope for a brighter future. How do you expect me to believe that my world, my life, and my future can be restored by trusting in a crazy dude on a cross who died because He was sent by some wizard or something to hang on a piece of wood? That is madness, just madness. How can I trust Him? How can I ever trust you now?"

When I turned to face him, there was no retaliation in the gaze he returned. The green-brown eyes were softened by tears that pooled but refused to make tracks down his face. He took my hand, making physical contact with me for the first time.

He kissed my forehead and gently said, "He loves you, Laura. He would never throw you out of His church. He will love you forever, just as you are. To Him, you are more than good enough. He just wants to love you. Don't take my word for it. Why don't you just ask Him?"

He turned and walked out the front door, closing it behind him with a barely audible click. I stood there feeling numb. "Why won't these people leave me alone?" I wondered out loud. As I locked the door, I realized Bob had left something on the phone table that sat by the door. It was a book.

"Oh great. Now I have to see him again, if only to return his forgotten property," I told my empty living room.

I picked up the book and opened it. It was a Bible. Of course it was. What else would he be carrying around, a travel brochure? I would have to drop it by his house or his work in the next few days. That's all I needed—more words thrown at me about this Jesus.

"Why don't you just ask Him?" Bob's words returned.

Ask who, this book? *Okay, let's ask,* I thought with the confident defiance afforded to those who know they are right. I had no idea where to start reading in Bob's book. I decided it was best to get a good night's sleep before beginning my wade through it.

I had another beer and went to bed. I fell asleep without much effort. In the early morning hours, I began to dream. In the dream, there were flashing lights and vivid colors running through my line of vision, like a melting watercolor.

As the abstract nature of the scene cleared away, I saw a little girl sitting on a metal chain-link fence. She was just sitting and looking up into the sky at two jet streams that crossed in the vast blue nothingness. Her lips were moving, but I couldn't hear the words that were coming from her mouth.

I was having difficulty breathing and felt pain in all four of my limbs. In the state of half-consciousness, I was aware that I was sweating and panting. I forced myself into full consciousness, or at least as close as one gets while engaged in a tug-of-war between a dream and the desperate fight to return to reality.

I fought the belief that I was having a heart attack or stroke. I sat straight up in bed and tried to convince myself I was too young for either of those diagnoses. Unfortunately, I have always had a propensity to go for the worst possible scenario and the highest degree of drama.

As a child, I was diagnosed with mild asthma. I was informed in my teen years that smoking could seriously compromise my health. My thoughts bounced between this predication from medical types and guilt brought on by believing that finally my Scottish/Irish-Italian temper really had caused me to pop my cork. I fought to find reason while waiting to see if my head would explode.

During this mental Ping-Pong match, the symptoms of shortness of breath and limb pain subsided. I was left wondering what I needed to do next. Would the pain and shortness of breath return? I fell back in the bed, drained and sweat-drenched.

"Why don't you just ask Him?" The words of my recent visitor echoed off the walls of my miniscule house.

Ask who? This "died for us" stranger? There could be no way. Why me? There was nothing special about me. Who was I to attract the attention of a man or God or whatever He was who would die for me? Why? Was it possible He knew me? Bob said so. No, it was impossible. It just could not be. It was *not* logical. Why me? Why would He, how could He, want someone like me?

I had led a life of violence and rejection from day one. I sought to escape it with alcohol, drugs, men, food, and whatever I felt could fill the void. My life was a mess, and I knew it. There was no way I was going to fit into the Bible crowd or the God-loving people of the world. Why did they keep coming into my life? What did they want? What did their God want?

"Why don't you just ask Him?" Bob's words were as clear as when he had spoken them the first time. I jumped and looked around my dark little bedroom, shivering and clutching my blankets to my chin.

"Stop it!" I screamed. "Stop it, and go away. I don't want you, and I know you could never want me. Not me, not really. Go away!" I was pleading and crying without giving myself permission to weep. All I wanted was for this nightmare to end.

I got up from my bed. I was relieved I could, in fact, get up. I walked through the house shouting at the air and darkness. No owner of the voice materialized. There was nobody. There was nothing. For the most part, the house was dark, except for a little night light next to the west window in my living room, by the phone table. It illuminated only one object. It was the book Bob had left behind. I picked the Bible up, turned on the small desk light on the phone table, and headed for a cold beer. Then I changed my mind. I got a drink of water, sat down, and began to read.

Bob had placed two yellow sticky notes within the text. I opened the book to the first note and read the paragraph it marked.

> He is despised and rejected of men; a man of sorrows, and acquainted with grief; and we hid as it were our faces from him; he was despised, and we esteemed him not. Surely he hath borne our griefs, and carried our sorrows: yet we did esteem him stricken, smitten of God, and afflicted. (Isaiah 53:3–4 KJV)

Questions floated through my mind like a PowerPoint presentation on fast-forward. *Who is rejected? Who knows the grief and sorrow? What about this language? Who wrote this stuff? Who could understand this stuff?*

I moved on to the second sticky note. It was placed at the beginning of the gospel of John. "Okay," I said, "I'm asking you, man."

For the next few hours, I read. Because it was Friday night and I didn't have to work the next day, I paid no attention to the clock. I had no need to rise from sleep early. This was an unusual Friday night, when none of my friends had been able to go out for one reason or another. I was alone when Bob arrived. I was surprised to see him because he had not stopped by on Fridays or Saturdays before. He had only visited on weeknights.

The language in the Bible was unfamiliar to me. The read was slow and tedious. Reading was not one of my shining points. I couldn't sit still long enough to complete reading assignments. My comprehension was assessed to be at the sixth grade level when I was a senior in high school. All the same, I sat still, I read, and I asked.

When I finished the gospel of John, I closed the Bible and focused on the light coming through a window, with the promise of a glorious Colorado sunrise. I stared at the light, and asked, until sleep finally agreed to become my companion.

CHAPTER 4

Help Wanted

I woke up in an armchair, at noon, with my neck all but dislocated and feeling like I'd been hit by a truck. I'd had many Saturday morning scenarios like this, but they usually followed a Friday night party. Even in my fog and disorientation, I knew I had not been on a party. There was something different here—something unclear yet enticing. I was thirsty, but I didn't have my usual headache after a night of, "How about one more round, boys?"

With no appetite, I chose to skip breakfast. Instead, I made a pot of coffee and went to wash my face. Looking in the mirror at swollen eyelids from crying and sleep deprivation, along with smeared streaks of mascara, caused me to take a step backward in shear fright. I made a note to purchase waterproof mascara the next time I bought cosmetics. I was a mess.

I spent the day trying to clean myself up and put some sense into what appeared to be the insensible, and somewhat alarming, events of the previous night. I decided not to go out of the house for a couple of days. My house was well stocked with beer, cigarettes, and enough food to accommodate that decision. I unplugged my phone to make the isolation complete. I don't know who I was expecting. But whoever it was—from this world or beyond—they were not welcome.

I refused to pick the Bible up again. It lay, benign but inviting, on the table by the west window. I let it lie and willed my eyeballs to behave in their sockets and not steal sideways glances at it. I wasn't sure I could do another solo trek into an emotionally charged quest for Jesus. I needed some help here—a guide, a companion.

Besides thinking of ways to keep my hands and eyes off the Bible, I had other issues consuming my thoughts. For example, I didn't know how to get Bob's book back to him with, hopefully, even a small amount of face saving. I also had to find a way to talk to Eric at work. My cool distance and frank ignoring of him probably needed to be addressed at some point. However, the most difficult issue I was wrestling with was how to find out more about Jesus and what He wanted from me.

On Monday, Eric avoided me. I couldn't blame him, and I wasn't sure what to say if we had spoken. I chose not to pursue a conversation with him. The first thing on my agenda was to find Bob and return his book. Ending my self-imposed hibernation, at the end of my work day, I began my search for Bob.

I went to the house he told me he lived in and knocked on the front door. A woman answered the knock. She was a small, round-faced woman in what I guessed to be her fifties or early sixties. Ah, Bob's mom. I hadn't considered that he had a mom. Of course, he had to have a mom. I just never entertained the possibility that he lived with his mother.

When she opened the door, I spoke first and quickly, reflecting my nervousness and maybe even some embarrassment. "Hello. Um, I'm looking for Bob," I said.

"Bob?" she asked. "I'm sorry but there is no one named Bob here. It is just me, my husband and our cat."

"There must be some mistake. You see, I met a man named Bob, and he told me he lives here. He was a young man in his thirties with brown, curly hair and was about this tall." I tried to put my hand up to where I thought Bob's head would be if he were standing next to me.

"I'm sorry, young lady. He did not give you the right information," she insisted.

"Are you sure, ma'am?" I couldn't believe I'd gotten it wrong. This was the house. I just knew it.

"I'm sorry. I can't help you." She closed the door.

Well, fine. I was wrong. There seemed to be a lot of that going around lately. I had moved from my family and a good income to the middle of a place where I could barely afford to eat and where people lived in a house one minute and disappeared the next minute. Then there was my judgment of my work friend, who I thought was judging me. That would have to wait another day or two.

I needed to figure out how to say I was sorry without admitting guilt. That was a well-tuned survival skill I mastered while learning how to stay alive in my family of origin. But, I was finding not much from those days was working very well in my new situation. I had never been good with apologies. I didn't know how to offer them now to Eric or to Bob.

As I walked away from the little blue house with no Bob, I reflected on the fact that I wasn't sure what I knew or what I didn't know. One thing was for sure: I did not want to lose these two men from my life. That disturbed me greatly. They were not lovers, bosses, or anybody I should be concerned with to this degree. But they were important to me. My discomfort around why they were important grew as I tried to process where Bob might really live. I knew how to find Eric. Bob was proving to be more difficult to locate.

I remembered Bob said he worked at a bar on Main Street. I set off to try my luck locating him there.

Bob's place of employment was what my father would call "a real dive." It reminded me of the multiple places we accompanied him to when he was searching for our absentee mother while she was on her drinking binges. I shuttered at the memory of sitting in the back seat of our car with my sisters and waiting in dark, cold parking lots while Papa went into place after place. He became more furious as each attempt proved fruitless. My heart hit the old speed bump that threw me into terror at the thought of what he would do to her when he finally found her.

"No," I sternly reminded myself. "Shake free, Laura. That was then, and this is now. She probably deserved what she got. No matter. No man will ever pound on me like that. Move on. It's over."

As I stood outside the small building, I realized I was a bar snob. I had my standards as far as drinking establishments went, and this one just didn't measure up. The place had only one door facing Main Street, with a sign that read "In and Out." Upon entering I was treated to the smell of beer, cigarettes, urine, and vomit. There were several elderly men seated at the bar, drinking beer.

A man came out from behind the bar and asked, "Can I see an ID please?"

I ignored his request and began an inquiry as to what time Bob came in. His response was the same as the lady in the blue house. No Bob. He had never heard of this man. His only cook was a woman who had been with him for two years. He told me that if I wanted to stay, I needed to produce an ID. I didn't want to stay, and I didn't produce an ID.

Well, there was no Bob at the little blue house and no Bob at the sleazy neighborhood gathering of old drunk guys. So now what? I figured I would just have to wait and see if Bob came back. I wasn't holding out much hope on that. If I had received a tongue lashing like the one I gave him, I'd keep my distance and find a safe place to nurse my wounds and well-earned grudge. But that still didn't explain why he lied about where he worked and lived.

This was getting harder and harder. I thought Jesus was going to make things easier. So far, it appeared Jesus and I had a little communication problem and a big difference in how we defined the word *easier.*

Feeling lost outside the bar, and no doubt looking that way too, I leaned against my car and breathed in the fresh breeze. Not only was the brisk air a relief to my assaulted nostrils, it produced feelings of calm and safety. I turned my attention to the dancing leaves in the gutter.

Despite my attempts to distract myself, the question still remained. Now what? There was no sense of urgency, just an overwhelming feeling that I needed to do something. I had no clue how to proceed. What was I supposed to do about Jesus, about Bob, or about Eric? Everything was changing fast and without anyone asking my consent. That annoyed me, because I was supposed to be the one in charge here.

I opened the door of my old Chevy and put the Bible on the front seat. As I closed the door and reached into my jacket pocket to pull out a pack of cigarettes, a five-dollar bill landed on the toe of my boot. Well, some things in my life weren't changing. I was still tucking money away in places and forgetting about it. That was a trick I'd learned by watching my dad hide money so my mother wouldn't spend every dime on the drink.

"Okay, Jesus," I said under my breath as I marched down the street toward one of my favorite watering holes, "I've no idea who You really are or if I can trust You. I don't know what You want, and I can't say that I want You. While we are on the subject, I'm not real crazy about how You introduced Yourself into my life. But come on anyway. I'll buy You a beer."

CHAPTER 5

I'm Sorry, I Think

Eric caught a cold and was off work for the next three days. On Friday morning at staff meeting, he didn't look in my direction. I noticed he was a little pale and seemed thinner. After the meeting, we each went to our respective assignments. He headed out the door before I could catch his eye.

I waited for him in the break room at lunchtime. When he walked in, I said, "Hi."

He ignored me and turned away.

"How are you feeling?" I pursued.

"About like I look, as if you care," he said over his shoulder.

Well, who could blame him? He didn't feel well, and I don't think it was just his physical body that was hurting.

"Hey, Eric, can I talk to you?" I asked. "I know we haven't had too much to say to each other lately, but I, well …" I suppose the word *please* would have been a nice touch, but it wasn't really in my communicative fund of knowledge.

"Not today, Laura, okay?" It was clear that he just didn't want to be bothered with me.

"Sure, okay. But when you get time, I, um, kinda wanted to ask a few questions about this guy we were talking about." I tried not to plead, but I really needed some help here. I assumed Eric was the person most likely to supply the information I was seeking. The last three days had been tough with no one to talk to about Jesus and failed attempts at wading through a book that made no sense to me.

"What guy? What are you talking about?" he asked. It appeared that his irritation was mounting.

"You know this one you were telling me about, this Jesus?" I knew I was getting nowhere.

The last few words fell out of my mouth and diminished in volume as I turned to leave the room. I realized my question was being met by his back. It seemed he had no intention of turning around or acknowledging my attempt at conversation, let alone engaging in dialogue with me. I was wrong.

"What about Him?" His tone was softer, and his irritation seemed to have lessened.

"I just don't know where to find out more about Him, or if I even want to find out more about Him. I guess I want to know what you do with this Jesus if, and only if—mind you—a person decides maybe there really is something to all of this." I was trembling as I spoke. I felt like a little girl trying to apologize for spilling food on her only good dress. My cheeks began to burn when I realized I was rambling.

"Well, I'm not sure I understand the whole question, but reading the Bible is a start," he offered.

I shook my head as I stared at my shoes. "I'm trying that, but I can't make any sense out of it. It's like reading Shakespeare or something. I mean I think I get the gist of the whole thing, but man, some of the details are just …" I trailed off, not able to complete my thought or my sentence.

"What version are you reading?" he asked.

"What?" I asked, feeling stupid. What did "version" mean? This was a mistake. I had no business trying to figure this whole thing out.

"There are lots of versions, translations, of the Bible," he told me. Was he trying to dumb things down for me? "Can you tell me anything about the type of Bible you are reading?"

"It's brown and all worn out," I said, thoughtfully recalling any available details but still not meeting his gaze.

"Okay. Is there a name or letters on the Bible?" he asked.

"Some king guy," I guessed.

"King James?" he asked.

"Yeah, that's it," I said. Ah, good—redeemed and feeling almost literate again.

"Okay. Well, that's a tough version for anyone to understand, even if you've been reading the Bible for years," he assured me.

"No kidding." I began to loosen up a little bit and raised my eyes to meet his. But my head remained lowered, like a turtle ready to retreat into its shell at the first perceived threat.

"Yeah, there are others that are easier to understand. Would you like me to bring one to you?" he asked. The kindness in his voice let me know there was a good chance I was forgiven without asking for pardon.

"I don't know. I think I'm just not cut out for all this religious stuff. I don't have a clue what I'm doing," I admitted.

He laughed, but not in a mocking way. He was making a genuine attempt at reassurance. "Who does? And it isn't about religion. It's about a personal relationship with Christ. You might think about going to church too."

"Church! Nothing doing. I am not walking into a church, ever." My voice was beginning to rise. At first, he didn't pick up on the fact that this was not a negotiable point.

"What is it with you and church? Whenever Len and I talk about church, you get up and walk out of the room. Why? What have you got against church?" His voice remained soft, as if he were speaking to a small child.

"Look, let's take one step at a time, okay? Will you help me with this Bible thing?" I needed his help, and this was the best I could do at trying to secure it.

"Sure, but I think you should—" He stopped speaking when I stood up straight and issued a cold stare in his direction. No on the church thing was the nonverbal message I was sending, and apparently he was finally getting it. I moved toward the door. I just wanted to finish my workday, go home, and be alone.

Hibernation was becoming a way of life for me, and I actually began to enjoy being alone when not at work. On the weekend following my conversation with Eric, I spent Saturday night at home. I didn't go out with my usual bar-stomping crowd. On Sunday, I slept in late, had a good breakfast, and took a walk. The silence and solitude were proving important in my quest to put pieces together around Jesus, what I was doing in Montrose, and how to handle my increasing job and financial troubles. I spent several hours that weekend thinking about Bob and hoping he would come back to see me. He didn't come.

Eric did bring a copy of the New International Version Bible to work on Monday and suggested I try reading it. He again encouraged me to consider going to church. I accepted the Bible but rejected the church attendance idea.

"Okay, okay," he said. "But if you change your mind, you might ask Len about his church. I live out in the country and my church might be a little far for you to travel." He spoke while issuing a shy, surrendering smile. For the first time, I realized I was attracted to him beyond friendship. Why had I not noticed that before?

"Eric, I want to thank you for your help. I know you mean well, and I'm sorry for my, um, um, behavior toward you. But please try to understand that this church thing is just not for me, okay? I can't explain why."

It wasn't a lie. I couldn't tell him what I had against church. I couldn't tell anyone.

He put his hands up in the air with his palms facing me. "Just a suggestion," he said with that same endearing smile.

This time, I smiled back.

CHAPTER 6

Mounting Evidence

I had a few more conversations with Eric. But our talks didn't shed much light on the subject of what to do with Jesus. He did ask me what had brought about my change of heart when it came to God issues. I decided it was best to keep the secret of my dream and the night of pain and sweat to myself. My trust only went so far, even with men. I didn't think anyone would believe me if I told them about the events of the night I'd first picked up Bob's abandoned book. I stayed up later than usual most nights, reading the Bible and trying to decide if indeed I had the guts to walk into a church setting.

I had once heard a psychiatrist, on a talk show, say that everyone dreams. He said we don't always remember our dreams, but we dream all the same. Well, he had never met me. To the best of my knowledge, I never had dreams. An exception was, of course, my deep-sleep trip down the modern art gallery that led me to pick up Bob's Bible. However, it appeared God, or Jesus, was beginning to use this particular medium in an effort to reach me.

One night when I retired and fell into a deep sleep, I had another dream. I dreamed about a boyfriend from high school. I had been out of high school only ten years, so thinking about my high school chums wasn't really all that unusual. But I hadn't thought about this boyfriend much since we'd broken up in my junior year.

We had begun dating when I was a sophomore and he was a senior. He was a popular kid, played football, and was involved in a lot of other activities in school. He was one of the guys the girls swooned over when he walked through the cafeteria in tight blue jeans and fitted short-sleeve shirts that showed his muscled, young body. He turned female heads from desire and male heads from envy and admiration. To top it off, he was a kind guy. He was nice to everyone, even the boys who tried to challenge him into fighting. By everyone's light, he was quite the catch. I never understood why he picked me to go out with during his senior year.

We dated through my sophomore year and part of my junior year. But then, because he was at college and I wanted to go out with other guys instead of just sitting around if he couldn't come home for the weekend, I called it off. We went our separate ways.

In my dream, I relived the day of my father's funeral. In the middle of my junior year, my father died from a malignant brain tumor. This ex-boyfriend came home from college for the funeral, even though we had broken up just a few weeks before my dad's death. He gave me something that day. But in the dream, I was unable to clearly make it out. I felt myself straining, in this dreamland, to see the item he handed me. It was of no use, and I slipped back into a dreamless dark.

In the morning when I awoke, I didn't go to the bathroom to brush my teeth or to the kitchen to put on the coffee pot. Those were my normal activities immediately upon arising. Instead, I went to a box of books I had brought with me when I moved to Montrose. I began digging through it at a furious pace. At the bottom of the box was a small, white Bible. Inside, my high school beau had penned these words:

> But as it is written, Eye hath not seen, nor ear heard, neither have entered into the heart of man, the things which God hath prepared for them that love him. (1 Corinthians 2:9 KJV)

I sat staring at the familiar handwriting on the front page of the little Bible. My ex-sweetheart gave me this at Papa's passing as a way of offering comfort in knowing my dad was in a better place.

If this had been a court case, there probably was enough evidence to bring in the verdict that Jesus was real and trying to get my attention. I examined all the facts. There was the presence of Bob and Eric, the first dream with the jet-stream cross, the second dream with the high school boyfriend, and the voice that ceaselessly told me God was always there. That voice had long ago taken a back seat to the tough upbringing of a child who felt unloved and unwanted by those around her and was in a constant state of trying to win approval and avoid harsh punishment, while learning to pick her way through a world that held very real opportunities for life-altering harm.

I held the Bible close and rocked back and forth while realizing that what Eric and Bob said was true. God loved me and had sought relationship with me all along. I now knew I was the little girl, sitting on the fence, in my first dream. God sent a sign while I sat there lonely and rejected. He placed, in my life, the most desired boy in high school. That boy showed me patience, kindness, and love. God, through my ex-boyfriend, sent reassuring Scripture at the darkest hour or my young life. My new friends and associates in Montrose continued to bring the message to me, despite my resistance and hostility. God chose to use only men to bring His truth to me. He knew I had no trust in women. Even that last detail had not escaped His eye.

"Oh Jesus." I breathed into the little Bible and asked, "You have tried all these years?"

He had been there all along. It was Jesus who protected me from some of the horrors that could have happened in the company of my parents' drunken companions. It was Jesus who brought me out of Denver and to this little mountain town to begin a new life. And it was Jesus who was calling me from dreams at night and friends' words during the day.

I continued rocking back and forth on the floor. I sat in a small patch of pale sunlight that promised to reveal full light in recognition of a new day. And I clung to a book that offered the exact same thing.

In the breaking of a new dawn, in a post-dream but now fully awakened state, I shivered in my thin nightgown as it became soaked with the tears of the first real gratitude I had ever felt. At last, through an overwhelming flood of recognition, I surrendered, fully embraced Jesus, and believed.

CHAPTER 7

Help Arrives

It became my daily ritual to read portions of the NIV Bible Eric had given me. He was right. This version was easier to understand. The more I read, the less difficulty I had in understanding the basic principles within the text. It felt like I had a chance to begin unraveling the mysteries of the God I was trying to understand.

Eric was respectful of my reluctance to attend church. However, from time to time, he opened the door on the subject until I finally asked about his church and how one might go about attending it. He told me that his church was in Delta, where he lived. It was about ten miles north of Montrose. My old Chevy was on its last wheels, so that was not an option for me. He asked my permission to tell Len that I might be interested in attending church. I granted it.

Len invited me to his church and said he and his wife would be happy to sit with me during the service. I told him I would think about it. I didn't know Len that well and wasn't sure I wanted to attend church at all, let alone go with someone who was little more than a stranger to me. Len didn't push it. I didn't bring it up again.

A few weeks following my conversation with Len, I went out with two of my party circle friends, Candy and Liz. While we were having a few beers and some cheese enchiladas, I casually introduced the subject.

I told them I was thinking of attending a church on some Sunday in the near future.

To my surprise, Candy said, "Yeah, we've been thinking the same thing. Both of us were raised in church, and to tell you the truth, we miss it. So far, we just haven't found the time to attend. We really don't know what is available here."

"So," I ventured carefully forward, "are you Christians?"

"Yes." Liz spoke up. "We've both been Christians since childhood."

Of course they were. The pattern continued. I was silent, nursing my beer and thinking.

My thoughts were interrupted by Candy asking, "Do you have a church in mind?

After staring blankly at her for a few seconds, I put it out there. "Yeah, I do. A guy I work with goes to a church here in town. Actually, they are meeting in a church that doesn't belong to them. But they are thinking of building a church of their own soon. I thought I might try that one."

Candy shrugged. "Why not? We could try that. You want to go this Sunday?"

I said, "Okay. Could you pick me up? I'll find out for sure where it is, and we can check it out."

It was decided. At least I wouldn't feel alone with some friends by my side, or so I thought.

But when we went to Len's church, I did feel alone. I felt very alone. Candy and Liz had grown up in church and seemed to be comfortable with everything going on. I felt like the proverbial fish out of water. I didn't understand the music, and had it not been for a printed piece of paper they gave me when I came in, I would have never managed to be on the right page in the red book they called a "hymnal." Liz had a beautiful singing voice and had no trouble crooning along with the other people. I tried to follow the proceedings but kept watching the clock and willing it to move forward faster. I wanted out of there, quickly. I didn't belong.

When it came time to put money in the wooden basket, I had none to give. Red faced and embarrassed, I passed it on. I leaned over to Liz and whispered, "Why do they want our money?"

"That's how they keep the place open and pay the preacher," she said.

"Oh." I hadn't considered that. More ignorance was revealed.

I looked around and saw men dressed in suits. There were beautifully fashioned ladies sitting beside them. It seemed everyone was married and had children. Candy, Liz, and I were the only single people there. Everyone looked so clean and holy.

They were all attentive and apparently in agreement with the pastor as he delivered a speech of some sort. I had no idea what he was talking about. Candy and Liz joined the camp of those in familiar surroundings by listening and nodding. I was isolated. I couldn't wait to leave.

I was relieved when the last song was sung, and people began moving toward the door. I knew I could never fit in here. I felt like a fool.

"Let it go, Laura," I said out loud, to myself.

"What are you letting go of?" Liz asked.

I shrugged and told her I just didn't feel right here. I didn't fit in.

"Haven't you ever been in church before?" She wasn't trying to make me feel ashamed. Yet I did feel ashamed.

"Yeah, I used to go with my mom once in a while. It was a lot different from this."

"Give it some time, okay? Just give it some time," she advised.

I liked Liz and Candy. They were very kind to me and seemed willing to help me explore this new world. Besides, they were great party mates. Even though they were women, I was willing to follow their lead on this one and give it a try.

As we were leaving, Len spotted me. He introduced me to his wife, Angie, and I introduced them to Liz and Candy. Other church members came over, greeted us warmly, and invited us to return soon. I didn't want to hurt their feelings, so I agreed to visit again. If I was right and I was not going to fit in, then my resistance to church attendance would be based on my experiences while trying to "give it some time."

After attending several Sunday services, Len and Angie asked me to accompany them to a Wednesday night Bible study. I agreed, more out of curiosity than anything else. The more I attended church, the less like an outsider I felt. I kind of liked the new people I was meeting.

Liz and Candy decided they would keep visiting other churches to see which one they liked best. I had no need to shop. For now, I felt comfortable right here. And, I felt I didn't have any idea how to select one church over another.

What harm could there be in going to a Bible study at someone's house? Besides, I reasoned, maybe it was time I tried to understand the Bible a little more in depth. I found it hard, on my own, to wade through and make sense of it. I believed that without more fundamental understanding and knowledge, there was a slim chance I could find the Bible relevant to my life. I agreed to go.

CHAPTER 8

Dolores, Like the River

The house Len and Angie took me to for the Bible study was up on Spring Creek Mesa, a little west of downtown Montrose. It was on a large piece of land that I later understood to be part of an acre. Initially, that terminology meant nothing to me, a city girl who had never been to a farm in her life. If I thought I felt out of place in church, it was nothing compared to how I felt in this house.

The place was gorgeous. All the furniture matched in rich reds, browns, and greens. There were pencil drawings and watercolor pictures in black shiny frames on the walls. The artist was fond of animals and birds. In the living room, there was the largest bookcase I had ever seen outside of a library. I had never read much except what I needed to read in school. But I always enjoyed looking at pictures in books.

As a child, I loved libraries. They provided a quiet escape from my noisy and dangerous home. Sometimes, when I visited a library, I'd try to find a remote aisle to sit in and pretend that was where I lived. The big shelves, with all their musty old books, protected and hid me. I could feel invisible there, and I was safe. This bookshelf transported me back to that safe place.

"Would you like to borrow a book?" A deep voice startled me, and I jumped. The voice's owner threw back his balding head and let out a laugh that extracted me from my self-consciousness. I returned his smile.

"No, sir. Thank—thank you," I stammered.

He put his hand out in a greeting and said, "My name is Trevor, and this is my house. You are most welcome. This is my playmate, Dolores. We have been married for a long, long, long time."

A petite, gray-haired woman appeared beside Trevor. She had a smile as broad as her husband's and a warm hand that guided me to an overstuffed chair. It was next to a coffee table that was home to a world atlas. She was giggling at her husband's remark. She said, "He makes us sound so old."

"We are old," he said with a great deal of emphasis on the word *are.*

"Would you like to sit here, my dear?" She motioned to the overstuffed chair. No one had ever called me "my dear" before.

"Well, ma'am, I like this chair because it looks like my feet will touch the ground." I hadn't meant to make a joke. I stopped growing at the height of four foot, eleven, so my comfort in furniture was almost always less than that of taller people because my feet dangled above the ground.

The gentleman roared with an infectious, hardy laugh, and his bride beamed at me. "We know. That is why we have this kind of furniture," she said while sweeping her hand around the room.

Why hadn't I noticed they were so tiny before? They were just like me. They had to find furniture that allowed their feet to rest on the floor too. The sensation I had that night was one of not only being welcomed but honored. I felt like I was expected. I felt like I belonged. They were delighted to see me and share their beautiful home with me. Best of all, I sat in a chair where my feet could rest on the floor. No one seemed to care that I was the only one wearing bell-bottomed jeans and a worn jean jacket; had long, straight hair; reeked of cigarette smoke; and was under the age of thirty. It didn't matter that I had no husband, no children, and virtually no knowledge of the subject matter.

After the hour-long discussion of Bible verses, Dolores said she would serve coffee and dessert. She disappeared into her kitchen. I rose quickly and followed her. I was afraid she would disappear into one of the large rooms and not come back.

She asked, "Would you like to help me serve the coffee and cake, my dear?" She busied herself at the counter.

"Yes, I would," I said.

I took the opportunity to survey the largest kitchen I had ever seen while I washed my hands. There were more cupboards than I could count and more of the same beautiful and unusual artwork on the walls.

"These are lovely pictures," I said. Had I just said the word *lovely*? I couldn't remember using that word before to describe anything.

"Thank you. My daughter is the artist. She is very good, isn't she?" Her smile widened, and there was something in her face I had never seen before. "We are so proud of her."

Ah, the look was of pride and love for a child. My stomach dropped into the pit of jealousy, although I didn't know at the time what it was. It was almost the same feeling I had when admitting to Eric that I was Bible ignorant. Not only did my stomach feel odd, but my heart hurt. I felt awkward and inadequate. I was back to not fitting in or being good enough to be in this company.

I distracted myself with a renewed survey of the kitchen and carefully rewashed my hands, hoping to remove the grime of not belonging. My hostess cut cake while humming some unknown tune.

The dining table, which sat at the far end of the room from where we were working, was a rich, reddish cherry wood and looked like it could seat at least eight to ten people. Six high-backed chairs surrounded it and were covered with white, embossed fabric. A vase filled with flowers stood in the center of the table. I had never seen a vase with flowers in it in real life, just in magazines.

I shuttled back and forth between the kitchen and the living room where guests were chattering. I delivered plates of chocolate cake and mugs of coffee to all takers. I couldn't make up my mind which I liked better: the dessert or the beautiful little dishes and dainty mugs. I didn't know they made dainty mugs. The little eating implements scared me, because I could visualize myself breaking a plate or spilling coffee all over someone, probably the pastor.

Some disaster was surely lurking, because my mother always told me I was the clumsiest little girl she ever saw. I tried to prove her wrong by becoming a cheerleader, pom-pom girl, and sort of an athlete when

I was in high school. I couldn't recall her ever noticing my efforts except to say the pom-pom skirts were too short. She told me that if I paraded around like that, it was my own fault if I ended up in trouble because some guy took me up on the message I was sending. It was years past high school before I realized what message she had accused me of broadcasting.

I never remembered her presence at a game I cheered at or a track or gymnastic meet I participated in. I was pretty sure that I hadn't just somehow missed a comment or demonstration of maternal pride where I was concerned. I pushed back the tears as I thought I would have given anything for my mother to say she was proud of me.

"Let it go, Laura. It's over. That was then, and this is now." I didn't realize I was speaking out loud.

Dolores said, "Pardon me. Did you say something, dear?"

I shook my head, subdued the blush on my face, and hurriedly changed the subject by complimenting her on how beautiful the cake was and how good the coffee smelled. She graciously stifled her curiosity and accepted the compliment with a wink.

"Well, when it comes to dessert, nothing beats chocolate."

She was right about that one.

When the last of the guests was served, Dolores asked me to sit down and join her at a smaller kitchen table, just us two. I couldn't take my eyes off her. Her short, gray hair was styled with a few little curls at the temples, and it shone in the overhead light. She had multiple freckles on her face and hands. Her twinkling blue-green eyes lived behind medium-thick, wireless glasses. She wore a white blouse that was buttoned up to her throat. There were delicately embroidered flowers on a front panel that hid all but the top button.

While we ate, she asked about my family, where I was from, and what I did for a living. I kept the answers lighthearted and benign. I had learned how to live stories as if they were true in an acting class at Colorado Free University, a year or two after high school. Concocting little harmless tales about parents and siblings took minimal effort. Over the years, I had become quite adept at carrying off this charade.

It seemed smart to paint my family as normal, ordinary, middle-class, hardworking folks with all the normal, ordinary, middle-class, hardworking characteristics the sitcoms of the '50s endlessly and expertly provided. Where I was from and what I did for a living were straightforward. So, of course, these items took less effort when fashioning replies.

For the rest of the evening, Dolores and I served the guests more portions of decadent cake called "double-death chocolate." If it was in the plan to construct a relationship between this dear little (five-foot, nothing) lady and me through my stomach, it worked. She did nothing to conceal her joy at my unladylike gobbling of more than one piece of her culinary offering. And I didn't think twice before accepting an invitation to dinner the following Sunday.

Before departing with Len and Angie, I thanked Trevor and Dolores for the evening. I wanted to remember their names. If I knew how to spell a name, I could remember it better because I made up a little rhythmic song with the letters. Each person had a different song. Once I associated the rhythm and music with their face, I could remember their name. Trevor's name was unusual, and I didn't think I would have any trouble with it. I had never met a Trevor before.

When I asked his bride to spell her name, her answer was quite deliberate. "D-o-l-o-r-e-s," she told me. "You know—like the river. My name is like the river in southern Colorado, my dear."

Trevor crossed his arms over his husky chest, threw his head back, and laughed from his belly. And Dolores, like the river, beamed at me.

CHAPTER 9

The Skeptical Heart

Trevor and Dolores took me from church the next Sunday up to the mesa for dinner. Still somewhat ill at ease in what I considered a "big, fancy house," I kept myself in check to assure I watched my manners, tried not to cuss, refrained from asking for any alcohol, and didn't spill the beans about my family background. After all, I reasoned, my chances of being part of this church crowd were significantly increased if their knowledge of my past was kept to a minimum. I figured my best course was to be vague or to actually lie. These were both skills I had refined long before my encounter with any of these folks.

My nervousness was unnecessary. My hosts insisted on serving me despite my protests and attempts to help with lunch. They asked very few questions about me or my background. They laughed and joked with each other, and Trevor called Dolores "Rosebud." These people were actually happily married. They liked each other. And they liked me.

I was mesmerized by Dolores as she moved around her big kitchen, humming an unknown tune and serving a luncheon she had prepared just for me to enjoy. I was so drawn to her that I began to be suspicious and told myself that nobody could be this good. At one point, I talked to myself while in the restroom. I reminded myself that even though

Dolores seemed to be a good person, she was in fact a woman. Her gender was her only downfall, so far.

After lunch, Trevor saw me admiring the atlas sitting on a table next to the chair I had occupied a few nights before. He asked if I liked to travel. I blushed as I told him I had never really been anywhere except for a trip to California once and Grand Junction a few times. I confessed I had always thought it would be wonderful to see the world or even just parts of the USA.

"Well, then, you are in for a treat. Come and sit here on the couch. Let me show you some of the places we have been," he said.

For the next few hours, I was given a glimpse into the lives of my new friends. Trevor and Dolores talked about their travels. They told me about places they had been and places they planned to visit. I was entertained with tales about different parts of the country and world, as well as some of the characters they had met in their travels. They showed me pictures of their two children and their two grandchildren.

They both shared some history of their upbringing, education, and occupations. Trevor was a metallurgist and had worked for US Steel. Dolores had been a schoolteacher in various grades. After visiting the Western Slope of Colorado one summer, they chose to make Montrose their retirement destination.

To my relief, they asked nothing about me, my family, or my background. I chose not to volunteer any information.

As evening drew near, I told them I needed to go home and get ready for the next week at work. They agreed to take me home, but only after I agreed to return for another meal in the not-so-distant future. No argument came from me. I nodded with unashamed enthusiasm that made both of them laugh with joy. What a warm, new feeling came over me as I realized that I had brought laughter to someone.

That night, I reflected on the meal and company I had enjoyed earlier in the day. I again smelled the scents of their lovely home. I felt the warm and genuine welcome extended to me by the home's occupants. I was certain that they truly liked me. But I was equally certain about how easily one can fall out of favor with family or friends, for no apparent reason. I knew approval was conditional. The trick was to find out what would make people like me. I noted again that Dolores was a woman, and women could not be trusted. I didn't have as much trouble being friends with men, so Trevor was not the issue.

I pulled myself up into a reality check by remembering who I was and where I was from. My lies about my life could fool others. But I knew the truth. I was encouraging people to like and accept me based on deception. I was not anywhere close to being the person they thought I was. As much as I hated it, there were really too many differences between Dolores and me for there to be a friendship.

Despite spending two hours presenting myself with the stark truth, I couldn't help wondering if I would find the courage to trust this sweet little lady with the ready smile, twinkling eyes, generous heart, and endless supply of delightful chocolate desserts. My mind told me it was not possible. But my heart wanted to believe it was more than possible.

I slept fitfully for a few nights as I considered that, in spite of and in the shadow of my past, there was an irresistible attraction to be part of whatever was going on in this church, and in this friendship that Trevor and Dolores were offering me.

The Stream of Relief

When the droplet collects more movement and strength, it forges a small stream in the yielding ground. The sweet persistence of the water provides opportunity for what was dry and parched to receive, and begin to crave, nourishment. This can provide a return to or the beginning of life.

CHAPTER 10

A Widening Heart

From my point of view, the ability to lead a dual life was not so much a gift but more like a necessity. In the company of my newfound church friends, I tried to say what I thought would be acceptable and upstanding. I lengthened some of my miniskirts and watched my language and taste in jokes. I brushed my teeth excessively before a gathering of the holy folk. I felt that smoking would probably prove to be a good reason for showing me the door.

It was perhaps the first time in my life I was grateful for being brought up by an alcoholic mother and a chronically raging father. I wasn't very far along in my childhood before I learned how to skate on the pond of what others considered perfection. By the time I was in my teens, I had learned the game of staying on the periphery of disapproval. Some days, being a master of this game proved to be vital to my existence. It wasn't always a guarantee that I would avoid excessive physical punishment and verbal tirades, but it lessened the chances significantly.

Since the death of my father when I was sixteen, the threat of being physically beaten had greatly diminished. The emotional abuse and ongoing disapproval continued from my mother, except in her rare periods of sobriety. The skills I learned for avoiding these unpleasantries were fairly well engrained and highly tuned. I was able to call these skills into use at will. Unless my temper got in the way, I was fairly successful at being whoever I thought others found satisfactory.

My temper and the understanding that I was entitled to the last word, as I was usually right, made my work world a living nightmare. I was frequently in disagreements with my supervisor and other workers at the facility. When I was offered another job, with more money and better hours, it took little effort to make the decision. Eric had moved five months prior to this time. Our relationship never went beyond a close friendship, but I missed him. However, I also realized he had to find better money to support his little one.

Despite time spent in church and with Dolores and Trevor, there was the spirit of a wild woman who lived in me. That spirit refused to be denied. I yearned for the bars, the dancing, and the nightlife that my friends in Denver predicted I would miss when the novelty of my chosen new life wore off. I felt lonely without my sisters. Although I liked Liz and Candy, it still was not easy for me to totally trust women. I yearned for male companionship and still preferred the company of men to women.

The degree of difficulty in finding male companionship proved high indeed. This was especially true because I didn't see any prospects within the religious circle. All of the men in my church were married. So that left the other half of the dual life—bars and parties—as searching ground.

To add to the confusion, I began to attend Bible studies on a regular basis. There was a sort of prescription in the Bible that talked about living life in a more pure manner. Admittedly, I was not sure how to go about that. The draw from my old life still outweighed the desire to fully embrace my new one.

I spent a lot of my free time with Trevor and Dolores. I enjoyed Trevor's high-spirited laughter and recollection of his life's tales. It was in Dolores's well-equipped kitchen where I learned secrets of making the vegetable concoction Trevor liked to call "G-4." This was an exquisite blend of farm-fresh vegetables that made a tasty drink with high nutritional value. I felt honored to have access to this coveted formula.

I also discovered how many ways an apple could be prepared and how to pick, cook, and freeze asparagus. The latter turned out to be a free-growing ditch weed that Trevor, Dolores, and I spent hours picking along the borders of the Olathe farms before the farmers eradicated this weed/vegetable.

I couldn't remember spending time with my mother baking cookies, learning recipes, or making any kind of meal. But in Dolores's kitchen, even in the hard work of canning and preserving foods, a deep bond was developing; it felt like we were related by blood. I loved our time together.

During our outings and meals, I began sharing my concerns for learning more about God's plan for me. Dolores gave me names of some of her favorite Christian authors and small books called "devotionals" for a more in-depth look at Scripture. I read these resources with curiosity, if not with a great deal of understanding.

I knew that in the company of these two delightful people, I could bring my questions, concerns, and Bible innocence without fear of impatience or criticism. In fact, the church I was attending had many loving, patient people like Trevor and Dolores. I just wasn't willing to expose my soft underbelly of spiritual ignorance to everyone.

I found I was as comfortable in Dolores's company as in Trevor's. Even though she was a woman, I was beginning to trust her. I looked forward to seeing her and sharing my new revelations, or confusions, about this man called "the Christ." Slowly, day-by-day, I fell deeper in love with Jesus and with Dolores.

In addition to spending hours in Dolores's kitchen, I was blessed to be a frequent dinner guest. It was not uncommon for Trevor and Dolores to include my friends Candy and Liz in the meal invitations. They were energized when surrounded by young people with our ideas and our interests. I was proud to bring my friends to what was increasingly becoming my home.

It took some time for me to relax when bringing my friends around for meals and other events. There were a couple of reasons for this. The uncertainties in behavior or circumstances from day-to-day, in my family of origin, made it risky to invite friends to my house. Additionally, my parents approved of few people outside of our family, so my friends never felt welcomed by them. There were a few exceptions, of course. But trying to separate those my parents liked from those they didn't proved to be too much for me in an attempt to avoid disapproval and berating.

One of Dolores's great gifts was hospitality. I continued to be mesmerized by this confident, vibrant woman who moved through her house and attended her guests with ease and a sense of self-worth that I personally had never known. I found her irresistible. She moved from task to task in no hurry, because she was busy pouring love into every delightful offering she extended.

I felt there was nothing I couldn't tell Dolores except, of course, my family situation. As my trust in Dolores grew, I began to open myself up to more in-depth relationships with other women. Liz and Candy became increasingly more important to me. I found I enjoyed their company and was for the most part trusting of them.

That, however, was not the case with every woman in my life. After a heated argument with a female office manager where I worked, I found myself unemployed. In order to collect unemployment benefits, I had to apply to three places a week and demonstrate I was actively seeking work.

One of my applications was accepted for a part-time job in a ladies clothing store. It was there I met a young woman named Carolyn. She worked in the store's shoe department. We were kindred sisters in the love of footwear. We enjoyed the slower times, in the store, when we could look at the latest shoe fashions, before they were available to customers. We were delighted when we were able to make purchases at substantial discounts.

It didn't take long to realize that Carolyn and I had many things in common. We were both single, enjoyed spending time out of doors, and liked eating at local restaurants. Carolyn was a Western Slope native, having grown up in a town called Telluride, about sixty miles south of Montrose. Most of her family lived in Montrose, and she had close relationships with her mother and sisters. She was proud to call me a friend. When she invited me to meet her family, they seemed to like me too. They asked for no explanations, and I gave none. It was a relief not to lie about who I was and where I came from.

Some evenings, Carolyn and I took sodas and an oversized bag of Cheetos and sat on the rim of the Black Canyon of the Gunnison. Carolyn became a confidant and a confessor. We shared secrets at the rim of the canyon while observing the Gunnison River flowing below us. We were like high school girlfriends, talking and laughing as we fought off the more than friendly squirrels who coveted the Cheetos.

I had always considered myself a city girl and would never have guessed I could be so enthralled with the beautiful country that spread out in all directions from Montrose. In those evenings, at sunset, we rested in the stunning beauty of the canyon. Through the lens of natural authenticity, I learned what Bob meant about the Creator Father's magnificent handiwork. Sometimes, when Carolyn and I sat in silence in this sacred space, memories of Bob surfaced. I missed him and wondered where he was. I had not seen him since the night I asked him to leave my house forever. I yearned to thank him for the many gifts he had given me, especially the worn little Bible he left as a guide to finding the Lord and, in many ways, myself.

I began to feel connected to the earth in a way that the city did not provide. This deepened my connection to God and to Carolyn. The earth connection reinforced what Bob said: "He made this all for us, because He loves us." In these evenings, in this place, with my new best friend, I felt special, loved, worthy, and grateful.

The sound of singing birds, rushing water, and softly rustling trees in the canyon freed me to be who I really was with Carolyn. With the backdrop of this raw, real, imperfect yet beautiful setting, I first began to accept that I was worthy of female friendship and that some women, in addition to Dolores, were worthy of my trust.

CHAPTER 11

The Secret Is Out

My loneliness had decreased greatly from what I felt when I first moved to this little town. But having friends was no substitute for having my two sisters around. When I lived in Denver, my sisters and I shared interests in concerts, movies, and plays. We enjoyed a variety of restaurants and took great pleasure in trying new foods. Most of the social things I enjoyed in Denver were not available in Montrose. Although I relished learning and doing new things in the country that the city couldn't offer, I longed to spend time with my siblings and enjoy our familiar pastimes.

The Christmas season approached. Liz and Candy said they were going to Denver to meet Liz's father. They asked if I would like to ride along and help pay for gas. They suggested it would be a great opportunity to see my family in Denver. Unfortunately, it was not possible for me to accompany them because I didn't have the money.

In conversation with Trevor and Dolores about my Christmas plans, I mentioned that I wouldn't be going home to see family. I told them I wanted to, but I was a little short of cash. Trevor didn't hesitate before offering me money to make the trip. I thanked him but declined the offer. I told them I could not see when I would be able to pay them back in the near future.

Trevor said, "This isn't a loan. It's a gift."

I blinked at him and again said, "No, thank you."

The hurt on their faces told me I had not made the best choice. After a dinner filled with unsuccessful attempts at making small talk, I asked them to excuse me because I needed to get home early. All the way home, I felt terrible for hurting their feelings. But my pride told me it was better this way. No matter how hard things got, I never asked anyone, even blood relatives, for money.

That night, my older sister called. She asked if I planned on coming home for Christmas. She said that she and my younger sister missed me and wanted to spend the holiday with me. I told her I was coming. After hanging up the phone, I called and asked Dolores if the offer was still open. She told me they would drop the money by my house the next evening. I thanked her profusely for the gift, and she thanked me for taking it.

The visit went well, and I enjoyed the time with my sisters. My mother didn't make herself available for the holiday, and I went back to Montrose without seeing her.

When I saw Trevor and Dolores shortly after New Year's Day, they asked me how my family was doing. I told them my sisters were fine but I hadn't seen my mother. The sadness in my heart felt too heavy to carry by myself any longer. After dinner, as we cleaned the kitchen and Trevor went to write letters, I made the decision to trust Dolores with the truth about my chronically drunk mother.

I don't know when the tears appeared in the course of my story. Dolores was silent during the oration. When I looked up at her, she too had been crying. I begged her not to tell anybody what I had just told her.

"I would die if the church people knew my mother was a drunk, a derelict, a skid-row resident. They all seem so, well, together and perfect. I think they would ask me to leave or something. I just know they wouldn't accept me now. Please, Dolores, please don't tell them."

Dolores said, "Honey, they are all far from perfect. We all are. I will never share what you have told me. Please, trust me on this and don't be anxious over it, okay?"

I wanted to trust her.

She continued. "I don't understand why you fear rejection because of your mother's drinking problems."

"Because I think sometimes she wouldn't drink if I were a better daughter." There it was. It was out.

I had never said that to anyone in my life. The shame of being the cause of my mother's drinking left me feeling panicked, short of breath, and unable to move. I wanted to hide under the table.

"No, Laura. That is just not true. You are not responsible for her drinking," she stated.

"Then why didn't she come to see me? She knew I was in town. My sisters told her. And why won't she stop drinking? She hates me. She told me once that if I were a better kid, she wouldn't have to drink!" I blurted out my confession of guilt.

"Oh my," Dolores said. "And you think that if the other church members knew about her problem they would blame you too?" She put emphasis on the word *her*.

"Dolores, I have worked very hard to be part of this church. I have done everything I can think of to fit in and be part of it. I don't want to get kicked out," I told her in a very soft voice so Trevor couldn't hear me in the next room. "If they know the truth ..."

Dolores interrupted me. "No one can kick you out of a church. God is the head of the church. Laura, He doesn't hold you responsible for your mother's actions. He will love you unconditionally forever, child. He will never kick you out of His kingdom, ever. You belong to Him. You are part of His family and ours—Trevor's and mine. You are definitely a part of this church community."

"Then why did the other church not want us because Papa married her?" I asked.

"What?" She shook her head in what appeared to be disbelief.

Oh brother, now I'd stepped in it. I took a big breath and told her the whole story.

"My father and mother married in the late 1940's. He had never been married before, and my mother was a divorcee. He was a first generation Sicilian-American, and she was of Scottish-Irish descent. Their ethnicity wasn't their only difference. They didn't share the same faith base. My father—"Papa" we called him—was asked to leave the church of his upbringing, because he selected a marriage partner who was divorced and not of the same religious denomination. Furthermore, she had no intention of converting to his denomination. My mother continued to practice within her own church but not on a regular basis. She believed organized religion was harsh and unfair. She saw herself and Papa as victims of that harsh unfairness. I also suspect that she was often too drunk to get up on Sunday mornings.

"Still, Papa was concerned for the 'souls' of his three little daughters. He wanted us instructed in the faith of his youth. I never saw my father walk into a church, but there was a big black book on our coffee table for as long as I can remember. I saw my father lovingly touch that book from time to time and didn't realize, until recently, that it probably was his Bible.

"The day Papa decided to present his request is a day that is permanently etched in my memory. He insisted we all wear our very best frilly dresses, polished little black shoes, white hats with pink netting, and our gloves. He scrubbed himself from head to toe and wore his only suit, complete with white dress shirt and tie.

"We went before the big shots of the church. They asked him if he was a member in good standing. He told them he was not but would like his children instructed in this faith like he had been when he was a kid. He was nervous and pleading. I had never seen my father like that before. Papa was a proud Sicilian man who had weathered the prejudice of Americans against Italians in the '20s to '70s yet fought in a war that pitted him against Italy—the land of his fathers. He was not asking for himself, because he said he knew he was damned, and there was no hope for him in the church or heaven. But he was asking for his three little girls—ages eight, ten, and twelve. The reply was swift and to the point.

"He was told, in front of us, 'We will not send your children away, Mr. Carvallo. But we think it best you reconsider their religious education. Because of your sins and poor standing in the church, we are not allowed to invite them to participate in the benefits of being in God's family. We do not recognize your wife's divorce and therefore do not acknowledge your marriage to her or your children from this marriage. There really is no place for them, and they do not belong here.'

"Papa did not argue but turned to look at his three wide-eyed, beautiful, hopeful little children holding gloved hands. With tears in his eyes, he replied, 'Thank you for your time. We will take no more of it.'

"We left that building and Papa muttered to me, 'Your mother may just be right about organized religion.' On the way home, no one spoke. I rode next to Papa as we four made our way home in his classic pickup truck. I kept looking at my Papa and wishing I could do something to stop the streaks of tears that were running down his cheeks.

"When we got home, Papa put his suit away. We never spoke of the incident again. I also never saw the suit again until the day we put him in the ground."

I stopped talking as a flashback of my father's funeral surfaced. I involuntarily jumped inside at the memory of guns firing in salute to my father, a veteran of war. The gun salute was part of his military funeral at Ft. Logan National Cemetery on a cold, cloudy February day in 1968. Later, someone told me that it had been a beautiful day with the sun shining the whole time we were at the graveside. I remembered no sun.

When I finished the story, I could not decide which was more intense: my sense of relief at sharing a shame I felt was mine alone to carry or the new sense of shame I bore for betraying family secrets. In my family of origin, family secrets were just that—secrets. Anyone revealing secrets would be considered a traitor guilty of treason, and treated accordingly.

Dolores's response surprised, and frightened, me. She spoke almost the same words as Bob. I sat in stunned silence for several minutes after she said, "Honey, God loves you no matter who you are or where you come from. He wants you in His house as much as He wants anyone there. To Him, you are more than good enough."

She went on to explain, "Churches are made up of humans. For the most part, church leaders do the best they can to be guideposts for us here on earth. But because humans are flawed, so are establishments we run sometimes. This includes churches and other places where people try to speak for or represent God. What happened was part of a man-made doctrine. Please don't hold anyone responsible. Try to understand they were doing what was thought right at the time, in that particular denomination."

Then I asked her something I have never asked another human being before or since. "Do you think my Papa is in hell because he wasn't good enough to go to church anymore?"

"Good Lord, no, Laura. No, absolutely no." She almost raised her voice, which for Dolores was unheard of. Again, she released the words in disbelief as she shook her head. "Oh, my. No, child, no."

After a few minutes of silence, she ventured forward, speaking very quietly. "How can you remember all that? You were only what—ten years old?"

I answered her question with a question of my own. "How could I ever forget it? Although I didn't understand all the words used or some of what happened that day until I was older, I will never forget."

"No wonder you feel the way you do. I'm sorry," she said, and I knew she meant it.

"You did nothing to be sorry about," I told her gently.

She asked me, "What did you do after you got home that day?"

"I changed into my play clothes and went to sit on the fence that separated our yard from our neighbors' yard. They went to church on Sundays and apparently were better suited to be with God than we were. I remember looking up into a sky I thought represented heaven and asking someone up there why we couldn't be in God's house too. I asked God who He really was. I saw two jet streams make an enormous white cross in the blue sky."

I remembered the dream with the running colors, flashing lights, and jet-stream cross. I shook my head to clear the memories and returned to the familiar warmth of Dolores's kitchen. "As the years went on and my family, well, it wasn't exactly ..."

No more details were needed. She nodded her understanding.

She asked, "You blamed God for your family situation?"

"No. Yes. No. Yes, yes, of course, I did. I do. I mean, look, I figured if He was going to ignore me, I would ignore Him. I felt like I never got an answer to my questions that day on the fence and that God, Jesus, and I really had no part with one another. That worked well up until now. Then you and everyone around me have shown me that He is exactly who He says He is. I keep hearing how much He loves me and ..."

I didn't know what else to say. I was struggling to talk as I released the tears of shame.

"Dolores, I sometimes don't understand what He wants," I confessed between sobs.

She sat back in her chair and looked at me. "It isn't about what He wants. It's about what He has to offer you, Laura. He loves you. He wants just to love you." The same words Bob had used. The same words Eric had used in some of our conversations.

"Sometimes, Dolores, I still don't believe that He would want me. I know now I want Him. I just don't know how He wants me to live my life and what He wants me to do with it. I just don't know." Forming my thoughts and getting them out was becoming difficult in this conversation. I felt like I had already said too much.

"Well, why don't you just ask Him?" she asked. My breath caught somewhere between the back of my tongue and the area where my tonsils used to reside.

"What did you say?" I asked. This time, there was no raised voice, no flashing eyes of fury, and no temper tantrum.

"Just ask Him. Prayer, Laura. You pray, and you ask Him to show you, guide you, and grow you in His way," she instructed.

I lowered my voice, looked around the room, and then whispered, "I don't know how."

There was a feeling in the pit of my stomach that was raw and irritating. It threatened to bring my dinner back to its original plate. I fought to keep myself from vomiting. I recognized the sensation as intense inadequacy and shame. It was beyond embarrassment. It seemed like I was confessing that I had no skills in this churchy, religious arena. I was a fake. I was faking it.

She leaned closer to me and asked, "Are you okay, my dear?"

"I ate a little too much, I think," I said, trying to reassure her.

"Nobody has a corner on the market when it comes to prayer. We just talk to God. Look, you are talking to me, aren't you? You are asking me questions, aren't you? Just do the same with Jesus," she said.

"I can't, Dolores," I insisted.

She asked, "Why not?"

"It's not the same, see? You are sitting right in front of me. I can see you. I can hear your answers. And besides, you fixed my dinner." I laughed in an attempt to introduce comic relief into a situation I had no idea how to get out of, or for that matter, stand in.

"He fixed more than a meal, my dear," she said, smiling at me. But the mist did not leave her eyes, or mine. I had nothing else to say. She too was silent and shook her head as she looked down at her apron, held my hand in hers, and stroked the top of it with her thumb.

That is how Trevor found the two of us when he returned to the kitchen. He said nothing but quietly turned around and returned to his work in the other room.

CHAPTER 12

She Was Right

I decided to take Dolores's advice and start asking God what His plans were for me. At first, it was awkward talking to someone I couldn't actually see. But as I read more in the Bible, I began to feel the words on the pages were God's part of the conversation between us. They didn't always make sense to me in terms of application, but Dolores helped me sort through some of my confusion and unsteadiness when it came to talking with or praying to God. And without seeing a firm line representing change, I began feeling His presence, even when I wasn't talking to or asking anything of Him.

I had no doubt that my secret was safe with Dolores. I don't know if she ever told Trevor. I do, however, know she was right about the church people. They included me and showed me love. They were tickled with my sense of humor. In previous conversations, Dolores told me it wasn't necessary to justify myself to anyone. I didn't need to retell my story. She assured me the Lord knew and loved me, and that was enough. She also said it might surprise me, someday, to find out others had similar types of stories. But according to her, I didn't have to tell everything to everyone.

Because Dolores was proving to be trustworthy, I began to have the confidence to trust more women in my life, such as many of the church ladies. I joined a ladies Bible study and still saw Candy and Liz regularly. I spent many hours in Carolyn's company. We talked and shared our dreams and hopes for the future while soaking up God's healing and wisdom that were reflected in His handiwork of the Black Canyon.

At first during my Montrose stay, I didn't go to Grand Junction to see my mother's sister, Fern. I had not spent much time with my aunt while growing up. My mother distanced herself from her family, which I assumed was because she married outside of her religion and ethnicity. I always figured her people didn't accept Papa, or us. So it seemed simple enough to just not accept them. But when Aunt Fern learned I lived only sixty miles south, she called and insisted I come for a weekend visit.

I agreed to go see her out of family obligation and because Aunt Fern was not someone a person opposed. She had owned and run a successful real estate business, was a strong voice in local and national politics, was used to being in charge, and had a way of making a request sound more like a command. There was little room for argument with Aunt Fern. Frankly, I was curious about this woman I had not known while growing up, and had heard very little about from my mother.

I decided to find out for myself who my mother's sister was. To my surprise, I liked Fern and enjoyed my time with her. After my initial visit, I often traveled to Grand Junction to spend time with her and my uncle in their glorious Victorian-style house. For the most part, our conversations were about my life and hers. We enjoyed shopping and making meals. She and my uncle were square dancers and ballroom dancers. I loved hearing about my aunt's passion for dance and seeing her costumes. And I was impressed that she personally designed and made most of her dance outfits.

Dolores was excited to hear about my adventures with Aunt Fern and details about her extraordinary life in politics and real estate. She suggested that on one of my visits I talk with Aunt Fern about my mother—what she was like as a child and a young woman. Dolores maintained that it might help me to know some of the good things about my mother as a young person, and as a woman. She said that God always gives us opportunity to live in health, but sometimes we need to do a little legwork on the path to finding that health.

Up to this point, Fern and I had managed to skirt around any topics that might lead to serious conversations about my mother. I figured good Christians didn't speak badly about others, no matter who they were. I believed if I ever started talking openly about Mom, my hatred would spew forth, and I would never be able to contain my wrath toward her again. I was afraid my mom would have been proven right in her assessment of me as a bad and ill-tempered little girl.

One night, my aunt told me that my mother and father had also been ballroom dancers. Taking Dolores's advice into consideration and seeing this as an open door, I asked what my parents were like when they were young.

Fern told me how my parents met and that my dad knew my uncle, her husband, because they worked together on the railroad. I enjoyed seeing my folks as young people with few cares, having fun and living a good life. Dolores was right.

After dinner, while Fern and I washed dishes, my uncle went out to his little backyard garden to do what Fern liked to call "pottering and puttering." I carefully introduced the topic of my mother's drinking.

"Aunt Fern, why do you think my mother drinks so much? Is she unhappy? Did she not want children? What is it?" I asked.

Fern took a deep breath, sighed, and said, "Laura, your mother, Audrey, was born before her time, and she was extremely bright. She wanted to be an attorney, you know. She had her heart set on law school and was a stickler for education for women. But we did not come from a family that could afford college, let alone anything beyond. We didn't have the right connections. Audrey and I were told by high school counselors that most women who did not get married should train for careers as nurses or teachers. Neither of these appealed to your mother. The counselors discouraged your mother from pursuing her dreams. I have always believed that is one reason she is chronically unhappy."

Fern went on. "It's no secret that your grandmother Fisher, Audrey's and my mother, raised us pretty much on her own. That was a bold and rare state of affairs for a woman in the 1920s and 1930s. Your grandmother married a man after Audrey's and my father died. Her second marriage was to a man she later divorced because he dared to raise a hand to her once. It was only once. She refused to tolerate any kind of abuse from anyone.

"Audrey went to work in a restaurant after high school, and that is where she met her first husband, Jerry. Our mother never liked him. I guess Granny Fisher saw Jerry as the same sort of man as our stepfather. She advised Audrey not to marry him. Unfortunately, your mother didn't see who Jerry was until she married him and they moved to New York City.

"They were only together a few years. By the time your mom came back home and divorced him, she was a wounded woman on many levels. Her drinking was out of control. I think in some ways our mother was angry that Audrey discounted her advice. And she may have even shunned Audrey for having tolerated the abuse for so long. She expressed relief when your mother met and married your dad. She hoped Albert could turn Audrey around."

My brain rushed to shut the floodgates to my mouth. It was not necessary for everyone to know everything. I chose not to tell Fern that my mother married another raging wife beater in my father. No, there was no need for that.

Fern continued to tell me how much everyone loved my dad and us kids. It was because of my mother's drinking and carousing that my grandmother and the rest of the family kept their distance.

"So," I asked, "it wasn't because my dad wasn't of the same faith? Or that he was a Sicilian man? Mom always said her people rejected her because they rejected him and the children she had with him."

"Alcoholics will say anything to get the blame off of them," Fern said. "You kids were and still are very important to all of us. After your father's death, I wanted to bring you girls here to Grand Junction to finish your education, because I knew your mother would not take care of you. But Audrey would have nothing to do with it. And you remember the day after your father's funeral how she threw me out of your house? That was because I warned her not to spend the money your father left on anything but caring for her children."

Well, there it was. No one in our family rejected us or Papa. The healing process had begun. I had had family all along. I was loved all along. No one blamed us for our mother's problems, except for our mother, of course. No one ever knew about Papa's abusive behavior.

When I next spoke to Dolores, she asked me how my visit with Fern went. I kept it light and benign. I was having a hard time processing all of this new information, and I wasn't sure how to verbalize what I had learned. I didn't have to tell everything to everybody, even when it came to this dear friend.

"You were right, Dolores. It was good to talk with Fern. She helped me see my mom, myself, and actually a lot of my family in a different light." I moved off the subject fast.

Dolores let it go. She knew I wasn't going to be forthcoming with details, and she would have never pressed the subject. I breathed deeply and thanked Dolores for her insight and good sense. And when I hung the phone up, I thanked God for Dolores.

CHAPTER 13

Just Like Everyone Else

Usually after our dinners together, Dolores and I would have a cup of herbal tea at the little table in her kitchen. It was the same table where we had first shared dessert. We talked about my job problems—and there were always job problems—my plans for the future, the last time I had contact with my family, or whatever was going on in my life. We never tired of talking about what God was doing in our lives personally and in our church family.

During one of our meals together, I opened up to Dolores about my loneliness and desire for a husband and children. Although my generation blazed a trail encouraging women to break from traditional roles of wife and mother (if that was their choice), there was part of me that still saw my worth defined by the loving husband, little family, white picket fence, and station wagon dream.

I explained to Dolores that I would feel more complete as a woman, and more a part of the church family, if I were married and had children. No matter how loved I felt, I had an empty feeling when I looked at the happy little families in our church. I imagined they all went home after worship service each Sunday to their nice houses and lived what I assumed was a reflection of families in the sitcoms I had grown up watching.

Dolores tried to convince me that my worth will always come from being a child of God. She encouraged me to be patient, pray, and wait on the Lord's will. She tried to convince me that being desperate for the things the world offered to define a woman could lead to disaster. I listened to her carefully and nodded my head in agreement. But when alone that night, I realized that in spite of the loving little church and these two loving new adoptive parents, I still was the one who went home alone. The ache was there for all the things I believed would make me whole. And despite the disaster that was my family of origin, I felt I could do a better job and build the perfect family, given the chance.

Because she was a fan of the psalms, she usually put one or two into our conversations. In this case, she quoted one of her favorite verses. "Wait for the LORD; be strong and take heart and wait for the LORD" (Psalm 27:14).

Patience is not one of my long suits. I rejected Dolores's advice to rest in the Lord's timing and employ trust and patience for His will to be revealed. Instead, I embarked on a course I felt would silence the relentless ticking of my biological clock.

There weren't a lot of single men in Montrose in those days. I can't say I aggressively pursued men, but I was not ruling out any possible candidates. Dolores stressed that it would be wise to find a man who had a similar faith base as mine. I really didn't see what difference that could make. Besides, all the men I knew in church circles were married.

I had become a master at living the dual life by now. I continued to frequent dance clubs, bars, and restaurants with my friends as well as participate in most of the church activities. I figured I was increasing the possibilities for finding a mate by trolling all sorts of waters.

A few weeks after my long discussion with Dolores about my future, I was having drinks with some friends in a local bar. I was introduced to a man I knew only by reputation. He was tall with a large build and dark hair. He seemed to be somewhat evasive. His name was Jack. I was intrigued by the mystery that surrounded him.

After our initial meeting, I saw Jack at various functions or dance clubs around town. I thought it odd that I had never met this man before or seen him in Montrose in two years but now I was running into him at various social gatherings I attended, outside of church functions. I noticed that he was always on his own when we ran into each other. He was usually charming and engaging while still managing to remain aloof and only slightly interested in me.

I was taken totally by surprise when he asked me out on one date and then several to follow. My interest in him grew, because he was different from anyone I had ever known. He was soft-spoken, and his demeanor was one that made me feel safe. Having come from a home where my mother was often beaten, in front of her daughters, I knew one thing in a man I wanted was gentleness.

His knowledge of literature, history, and the arts was far above mine. I was enthralled with his conversations on those subjects. He encouraged me to read books like *The Old Man and the Sea, Cannery Row,* and *The Grapes of Wrath.* He felt that reading would help make up for the poor education I had in the literary classics. I wanted to please him by being able to contribute to conversations about things that interested him.

This proved to be a labor-intensive endeavor because of the challenges I faced with reading. I tried hard to read the assigned books and not be too hurt at his criticism when my consumption and comprehension were slower than he thought acceptable for someone my age. I figured he was just impatient for me to get to his level. Since he was always reading a new book, I often felt frustrated that I could never really catch up. Still, I read, I tried, and then I tried harder.

We rarely, if ever, discussed faith. At one point, however, he told me that he didn't object to my beliefs and thought Jesus was really a good guy. I took comfort in this statement. It was his personal feeling that the people who believed in Jesus would definitely be with Him someday. According to Jack, Jesus would someday collect His faithful followers just like the other gods would collect theirs. This made sense to me and sounded like a reasonable compromise. Besides, I knew I could win him over for Christ.

As I spent more time with Jack, I found less time to spend with Trevor and Dolores. I missed them and wanted Jack to get to know and love them as I did. When I introduced him to them, they offered him the same warm welcome they showed to all my friends. Their approval was important to me, and I chose to see their friendliness toward him as an indication that they sanctioned this relationship.

The leaders of the little church I was part of decided it was time to construct their own building instead of meeting in another church's facility. Jack was helpful in this area because he knew who to contact for various permits and how to find laborers for jobs the men of the church were not able to do. I took this to mean I was right, and Jack was warming to the idea of being part of this church body and accepting Christ.

Jack and I were in relationship for only a few months before difficulties began to arise. We wanted different things and had different values. Additionally, I was not comfortable around his mother. During one of our dinners with Trevor and Dolores, tension that remained from a recent conflict was evident. It made for a strained and awkward evening. Jack was silent, and I was overcompensating with nervous and irrelevant chatter.

However, by my way of thinking, God must have been getting pretty tired of listening to me whine about being alone. I reasoned that Jack had been sent to fill the hole in my heart and help me construct a family according to the images I refused to relinquish. I believed this was God's answer to my prayers, and I was determined to be married by the end of the year. I wanted a family, period. And Jack's parents were pressuring him because they wanted grandchildren.

Having a family was another area of disagreement between us. Jack said he wanted kids but was in no hurry. I felt the need to start a family soon, as I was nearing the age of thirty. I put the thoughts about this difference on hold because I knew I could change his mind once we were married.

When we announced our engagement, Dolores was less than overjoyed. I became extremely annoyed with her and decided to address the issue when we were alone. I tried to convince her that this was what I wanted. I informed her that I loved this man. I told her that even though we had our differences like religion, kids, money, and future careers for each of us, love would help us make a happy life together. I did my best to make her see this was a good fit for both Jack and me. My tone and body language clearly showed anger and even animosity toward Dolores for the first time in our relationship. I demanded to know what she had against Jack.

She listened to me and then, with her eyebrows furrowed, she peered over her rimless eyeglasses and said, "I have nothing against this young man of yours. He is a very nice young man, with good employment possibilities. We have been impressed with the way he helped us get some of the building done on the church. But I am concerned that you are marrying for the wrong reasons, Laura. Could you be a bit more patient? Give it more time and make sure."

I was livid. How dare she deny me this chance at happiness and fulfillment? "I want to feel like I am part of a real family for the first time in my life," I spewed out.

The blow was unexpected, and she reeled back as if I had struck her. I hadn't thought how my words would affect this woman who had come to introduce me as her surrogate daughter. Her eyes filled with tears, and I readied myself for retaliation.

Instead, Dolores gave a strained smile and said, "I want you to be happy, dear. If this man makes you happy, and you want to go forward with this marriage, then Trevor and I will support you in any way we can. I love you."

She took my hand in hers and patted it. We never spoke of it again.

Several nights later I had a dream. It followed a heated argument Jack and I had concerning wedding plans. In the dream, I was running in a wedding dress from a ball of fire. The fire eventually caught the lace on my dress and began to burn me. Soon, in the dream, I was consumed by the ball of fire.

By the time I shook myself awake, the only image remaining was of a fireball with lace and limbs protruding. I woke up sweating, panting, and with my head pounding. I found that the fireplace in my apartment had smoldering embers from a fire I had built earlier. Although unable to totally discount the dream as a warning, I eventually chose to believe it was the result of breathing smoke from the fireplace. I told myself I was just suffering from pre-wedding jitters in addition to the smoke inhalation.

As the wedding plans progressed, Trevor and Dolores offered to buy my wedding dress. Instead of a traditional bridal gown, I chose a plain suit with a cream-colored skirt and coral velvet jacket. Jack's mother wanted me to wear a long, flowing, white gown with lace. I wouldn't go anywhere around long, flowing, lacy gowns for reasons I refused to explain. There was a not-so-friendly disagreement. She was worried that her friends and family would think her son wasn't marrying a virgin. He wasn't. I stuck to my guns and wore what I pleased.

It wouldn't be the last time this woman and I stood in intense opposition.

Trevor and Dolores sat in the honored place of family, alongside my sisters, in the little church we had built. Trevor gave me away, and the family pictures included them beside Jack and me. At last, I had the "happily ever after" scenario I had craved.

My mother didn't come to the wedding and didn't even know about it. She had moved to Booneville, Arkansas, a few months earlier to be with some of her drinking buddies. Trying to get a hold of her proved to be impossible.

"It doesn't matter to me if she is here or not," I told myself. But the habit of being a good liar was beginning to lose ground. In quiet moments, I admitted that Mama's move to Arkansas was just another form of abandonment. On good days, it didn't make its way into my conscious thoughts. On bad days, I chided myself with statements like, "You really are a stupid person. Why did you ever think she would be here for you, for any reason? Grow up, Laura."

On my wedding day, most of the people I considered my friends and family were present. There was no need for a mother who didn't want me and no room for her in my new life. Mama was done causing pain in my world.

"That was then; this is now," I assured myself as Jack and I loaded up our little Datsun 280 Z with wedding presents and headed happily into the new life I had ordained.

If the courting had been riddled with strife, it was nothing compared to the conflict within the marriage. I did my best to keep my disappointment and unhappiness from Trevor and Dolores, even to the point of restricting my visits to them after the wedding. Since Jack accepted a job out of town about sixty miles, in a town called Gunnison, I told them the distance made it difficult for frequent visits.

We did visit Montrose on a regular basis, however, because my husband's parents were there. But we didn't always go to see Trevor and Dolores. We seldom visited the little church where we had been married. And although in our new location we had spurts of church visitation, the pattern of our lives fell more into the party camp than the religious one. We spent most weekends drinking and partying, whether we were in Montrose or not.

On the rare occasions when I talked to Trevor and Dolores on the phone or they made a trip to Gunnison to see us, I was vague about answering questions concerning attempts to find a new church home. Jack was tolerant of their inquiries but just as vague as I was. It was a topic we four soon stopped discussing.

One night, after we had eaten dinner at our favorite restaurant in Gunnison, Dolores patted my hand and said she was glad I was so happy and that things were going well. She truly seemed pleased for me. How could I confess to her that I now knew she was right? I had made a mistake. My marriage was riddled with strife and fighting. I was a frequent target of criticism and unkindness from my mother-in-law. When I asked Jack to defend me from his mother, he said I probably did something to provoke her outbursts. He felt I needed to give her more time and try harder to get her approval. So I kept my hurt to myself, waited, and tried harder. But, it was becoming clear to me that instead of this union being the answer to my emptiness, it served to confirm that I couldn't do anything right. I felt I wasn't worthy of love after all.

When I discovered I was pregnant, I was overjoyed and believed this was God's way of answering my prayers to help Jack and me work through our marital problems. I couldn't wait to share the news with family and friends. There was no one in our family more excited about the birth of this little one than Dolores. Our trips to Montrose grew infrequent as the time for my delivery approached. But Dolores and I made sure we talked at least once a week on the phone.

When my son, Gabriel, was born, I was certain that whatever problems Jack and I had would melt away and we would be the little happy family I had always envisioned. I was wrong. We both loved our son more than anything in the world. But the problems between the two of us mounted.

We attempted to patch things together by moving to the Denver area for a better job for him. We had accumulated a massive amount of debt, and I attempted to help financially by working two jobs while caring for a toddler. Our busy schedules left little time for Jack and me, as a couple, to work on problems within the marriage.

After several failed attempts at marriage counseling and separation from church support, the future for Jack and me was uncertain at best.

CHAPTER 14

We Make Mistakes; We Are Not Mistakes

What causes a couple to divorce? Maybe it is because of money issues, dissimilar values, or different wants and expectations from life. Perhaps, it is due to the baggage both bring into the relationship. These were questions I repeatedly put before God. No one wants to dissolve a marriage, and no one wants to hurt their children by putting them through that kind of emotional scarring process.

I sat once again at Dolores's kitchen table, now with my beloved small child asleep on the living room couch. Trevor had carefully placed a fleece blanket over Gabe and kissed me on the forehead before he left the room so we ladies could be alone. Dolores poured each of us a cup of herbal tea. I poured out tears of shame and regret laced with self-pity.

"Dolores, I am so sorry. I have made a mess of everything. I have hurt my child, my husband, you and Trevor, my sisters, everyone. Mostly, I let God down. I am so sorry."

I wept uncontrollably, rolling in the shame of knowing I'd blown it. I had thrown my life into turmoil and was sure I was responsible for ruining the lives of those closest to me.

Dolores said nothing for a few minutes. Then she furrowed her eyebrows, looked over her eyeglasses, and asked, "Why do you take total blame for this divorce?"

I couldn't understand her question. Of course it was my fault. Jack said so. His family said so. It had to be true. He was a really nice guy. How could it have been his fault at all? Then there was my temper and the fact that my education was so limited I was unable to sufficiently contribute to the family income.

When she saw my confusion, Dolores lowered her voice and said, "There were two people in this marriage, Laura. You have a habit of taking responsibility for things that are not totally or not at all of your doing. Remember when you were convinced that your mother's drinking was your fault? Remember your surprise to learn that your mother's family did not reject you, your father, and your sisters but your mother's drinking?

"Jack has his share of the blame too. When you first told me this was who you wanted to marry, I had my concerns. I always believed him to be an okay person. But your values and goals were totally different. And I could see you trying to change him into what you wanted him to be and vice versa.

"I know this is not what either of you wanted for yourselves or for your son. You said you and Jack tried everything to avoid taking this step. Divorce is awful for all concerned, especially for the children involved. There is no doubt of that. Now you must make every attempt to give Gabriel the most normal life possible. Families today come in all shapes and sizes. This isn't the 1950s. Still, it will require that both of you are in his life and let him know, on a daily basis, he is loved. Mostly, he needs to know his parents' separation is not his fault."

She waited a few moments to allow her words to soak in. Then she continued. "It will also require that you try to be your healthiest emotionally, physically, and spiritually. You can't do that if you take on all the blame and responsibility here. The mind-set of guilt will leave you unable to heal and move forward. You must learn to forgive yourself and forgive Jack. Laura, you need to understand and accept God's forgiveness. That is the beginning of healing, wholeness, and health."

I looked at her through eyes swollen half-closed from nonstop crying. Was she kidding? This is not what I expected, even though I had come to see this woman as a loving presence in my life. In my family of origin, a mistake was an excuse for blame, shame, and an avenue for being beaten up on many levels. Forgiveness, especially of oneself in a situation of failure, was not a familiar family dynamic.

I expected an "I told you so" response from Dolores. But instead, I found a woman not afraid to stand with me in the pain and to speak what she considered the truth, in love. She cried too and said she loved me and God loved me more than ever. Dolores's soothing words were the balm I needed to begin forgiving myself. She assured me that Jack and I were good people who just married under various pressures applied by our culture, small-town attitudes, and family. She reminded me that God had blessed us with Gabriel, our precious little one. Dolores was offering to me an example of true friendship and unconditional love, even in the face of a failure authored by refusal to listen to, and heed, God's warnings.

I went into the living room and lovingly stroked my son's hair. Dolores was right. Gabriel was a blessing beyond anything I could speak. I kissed his forehead and then returned to the little table in the kitchen.

It was there, in the familiar space I called "home," surrounded by the fragrance of rosebuds and soothed by cups of hot herbal tea, that God, Dolores (like the river), and I set about putting my shattered life back together.

CHAPTER 15

Then and Now

The stresses of being a single parent and working three jobs took their toll in a short period of time. I felt guilty because Gabriel would cry for his dad and ask why Daddy didn't live in our house anymore. He more often than not wanted to be with his father, even on the weekends when I had him with me.

One of the factors in our divorce was the financial stress Jack and I had put ourselves under while trying to build the perfect life. My share of the bills totaled more than my income, and I was usually behind in making payments. I knew it was just a matter of time before I would have to sell our home and move Gabe and me into a smaller and more affordable place. The real estate market in our area promised that at best we would break even on the house. There was no profit to be made. I feared that I wouldn't have enough money to put a deposit on anything, even if I could find an affordable alternative.

There were days when I felt hopeless, helpless, and angry about my situation in particular and life in general. I felt the people I trusted and cared about most, and maybe even the God I claimed to follow, had abandoned me. There were times when I felt I could not go on any longer. It never failed that, in those dark times, a letter would arrive from Dolores with a Scripture verse included. One of her favorites was

Psalm 34:18, which says, "The Lord is close to the brokenhearted and saves those who are crushed in spirit." I clung to that verse in particular. I copied it on a small piece of paper and read it several times a day. The verse, and the practice of reading it, helped me focus on living just one more day, for my son.

I did try to keep enough money out of the compulsory expenses to visit Montrose two to three times a year. Dolores was one person I still felt I could trust and confide in. She offered no advice unless specifically asked. She knew not to offer money, because I had refused it in the past. Pride and a need to prove self-sufficiency prevented acceptance of financial assistance. I dug myself into this mess; I could dig myself out. All I needed was to work harder and to be frugal with spending.

One afternoon while Gabe and I were visiting Trevor and Dolores, I was particularly angry with Jack, with me, and with the world. Dolores asked me if I had considered counseling or a support group for people who had grown up in dysfunctional and/or abusive homes.

When I indicated that I really had no idea what she was talking about, she said, "Well, it might be a place for you to start sorting out feelings about..."

"About what, Dolores?" I interrupted her in midsentence.

"Laura, I just think that the problems you had with your family of origin might be contributing to your anger and low self-worth today. By your own admission, Jack said your temper was one of the reasons that he felt he did not want to be married to you any longer."

Dolores was breaking from her usual pattern of not offering advice unless asked for it.

What she said was true. My temper and inability to control it was a big factor in Jack's decision to leave me. He wanted custody of Gabriel, because he feared for our son's safety.

"Dolores, I appreciate your counsel on this, but what happened in the past is in the past. It has nothing to do with today. The problems with my mother are behind me. I don't see how revisiting all that stuff will help me to move forward in my life now," I told her.

She smiled and said, "I understand, my dear. How about if we get dinner for Trevor and Gabe before they come in from riding the lawn mower around the yard?" She moved off the subject and onto the matter at hand: feeding our hungry men. She began to hum her unknown tune, and the subject was dropped.

Dolores's introduction to the topic of finding help, for exploring my past, stayed with me that weekend. And her concern about my anger reinforced Jack's feelings on that issue. I couldn't imagine abusing my son or losing control to the point of hurting him. But perhaps there was something in what Dolores said about flushing out the components in my yesterdays that contributed to my inability to be happy today.

On the trip back to Denver, I prayed that if there was something to Dolores's suggestion, God would reveal it and lead me to find out more. I tried to convince Him, as I had Dolores, that my past had nothing to do with my present.

Upon my arrival home, there was a phone message from a friend. She said she had been thinking about me and asked how I was doing. She asked if I had given more thought to her suggestion of going to a group therapy session to deal with my issues around my alcoholic mother. I had forgotten about her offer as well as the fact that she herself had found what she called "healing" in a recovery program. I put Gabe to bed, sat listening to the message over and over, and then realized God had once again provided a clear directive in response to my petition.

When I first walked into the rooms of a recovery group, I was stunned to find there were people like me who had lived with, dealt with, and suffered under the disease of alcoholism in a loved one close to them. After just one session, I knew I needed what this group was offering.

These group sessions, and the people I met there, became paramount in my personal journey to find an understanding of my mother's disease. For the first time, I had a realistic picture of how alcoholism had affected me. As a child, I had no choice over the behavior of others or the effects their behavior had on me. But in therapeutic recovery sessions, I began to see that I had nothing but choices around whether or not I wanted the issues of others to continue affecting my relationships, my work, and my life.

In those sessions, I learned to accept the fact, and speak it out loud, that my mother was an alcoholic. I learned that her behavior had planted deep seeds of mistrust, anger, and low self-esteem in me from an early age. I heard stories of similar abusive and negligent parenting. I saw hope for recovering from the abuse and negligence. And I remembered Dolores's words from a prior conversation. She had once told me that someday I might find there are people like me who share a similar background and similar experiences of growing up in a dangerous and dysfunctional home.

The fact that my father also had a drinking problem surfaced as I heard and shared stories. I had only seen him as a man who was angry with his wife for running around on him and had taken that anger out on whoever was around, including my sisters and me. I learned that his anger was deep-seated, and his own diseases of alcoholism and codependency fueled his uncontrolled temper.

His rage had been unleashed in the form of severe physical abuse toward his wife and children. Others in my group told similar stories of physical cruelty and punishment. I began to see that the beatings my father delivered to my mother and us were not mediated by anything we did and that no one deserves physical violence directed toward them as a means of discipline or conflict resolution.

Although I'd made up my mind years before I began dating that I would tolerate no abuse, of any sort, from a man, the inventory of my life events revealed that I was chronically frightened and perpetually angry. Until I began to sort through damages done, I was not able to understand my anger, let alone begin to channel it appropriately. I saw that I was at risk of becoming the abuser myself and admitted that in some ways, although not physically, I had done just that in many of my relationships, including my marriage.

Additionally, because I didn't feel I deserved to be treated with respect and dignity, I allowed myself to be treated poorly by others. By giving permission for this mistreatment, I had authored more of my own resentment, more anger, and more unreasonable outbursts of temper.

My counselors emphasized that the identification of my parents' illnesses was in no way an excuse for their behavior. But it was the beginning of understanding that they were as sick as any person with a physical ailment. They told me that no one volunteers for or chooses to have cancer, diabetes, or a myriad of other diseases that ravage the human body. And my parents did not volunteer for or choose to be alcoholics. I had always thought that my mother could have done something about her alcoholism. That may have been true. But the disease held a stigma in the '50s and '60s that made it humiliating to admit the problem, let alone seek help for it.

It was a pivotal step in my recovery to learn the disease was not a choice on my parents' part and, in some ways, was not their fault. More importantly, the shackles of responsibility I had carried my whole life for my parents' problems were released when I embraced the understanding that I was not to blame for their issues either. My only responsibility was to find a way to stop the patterns of behavior and the attitudes authored by the effects of their disease. Knowledge about their disease was the first step in that process.

The recovery took work. It was hard, painstaking, heartbreaking, and committed work. The healing was supported by group. But recovery was dependent upon the honesty of each individual in that group and the desire to truly change patterns, lifestyles, and attitudes. In the deepest part of my soul, the recovery instilled the need for, and gave the tools for, forgiving myself and others. It was the toughest work I have ever done. It was the most sacred work I have ever done.

Dolores stood at the ready to listen to whatever I wanted to share with her about my work of sorting out and letting go of my past. At least twice monthly, I received letters from her with Bible quotes. The quotes were reminders of God's love for me and assurances that He could be depended upon to guide me, through my heartbreak and healing, into the health He had to offer.

When we talked on the phone, Dolores never failed to ask about my progress. Sometimes, I was positive. Sometimes, I was negative and discouraged by the deep stuff of the work. Each time, the conversation ended with Dolores assuring me, "Laura, we are here whenever you need us and for whatever you need. We pray for you, Gabe, and Jack. Just keep working, keep reading, keep going to your sessions, and keep praying. Mostly, remember that in our weakness, we see His strength."

She encouraged me to read about some of Paul's struggles chronicled in the New Testament. She said that characters and stories in the Bible are there not only as a way of knowing God but of seeing how other people, even in ancient times, struggled with the same sorts of things we struggle with today. More importantly, she told me that the stories and people in the Bible are given to us as examples of God's faithful deliverance.

I did keep going to sessions. I read recovery literature and my Bible daily. I became familiar with many of Paul's stories, especially where he discovered God's strength in his human frailty and weakness. And I did pray. Oh, how I prayed. Finally, I surrendered my past, my pain, my failures, and my future to the God who offered me forgiveness and showed me how to forgive myself and those who had hurt me.

CHAPTER 16

The God of Second Chances

In the years following my divorce, Dolores and I often discussed the saying "Once burned, twice shy." I told her I never wanted to marry again. In her usual manner, she listened without judgment and offered no advice, but she did say I might change my mind if I met the right man. Still, I was full of uncertainty and skepticism. I didn't want any man in my life other than my son, who I saw precious little of due to all the jobs I was working while trying to pay off bills.

I told myself, and others, I had no interest in moving on in the romantic arena. But, despite my tough outer shell of independence, I sometimes felt lonely. And from time to time, the "less than" feeling crept in and told me a woman needs a man in order to feel whole.

Dolores didn't stop sending encouraging notes. They arrived almost weekly. On my birthday, she sent me a card, and after signing it, she wrote, "'For I know the plans I have for you,' declares the LORD, 'plans to prosper you and not to harm you, plans to give you hope and a future'" (Jeremiah 29:11). I memorized this verse. I prayed it daily, and I began to live a life reflecting belief in it.

Eventually, I stopped feeling lonely, because I believed God had a plan for me. Even if that plan included being without a husband for the rest of my life, I would be fine. I found a freedom from seeing myself as "less than" without a man in my life. I found peace in forgiving myself for being human, making mistakes, and having flaws. With God's grace, I was standing on my own two feet and not only paying off bills but putting money away in savings. Most importantly, I had more time with and for Gabe, because I was able to work fewer hours as the financial debts lessened when I sold my house and moved into a small apartment.

The healing I received, as a result of the work I did in the recovery program, allowed me a healthier outlook on life. I took a positive step in reshaping my future by enrolling in school. I had a good income and was making contacts to start my own home-based business.

I joined a church. Although I didn't initially feel as much a part of this faith community as the one in Montrose, I was able to carve out a little niche of belonging. I found other singles to mingle with and one or two women who were single parents and raising their kids while holding down full-time careers. I enjoyed the potluck suppers, social events, and Bible studies.

It was in a Bible study where I met Keith. After our initial introduction, I saw him from time to time around church. I noticed that he was almost always alone except for a young man, his son, who accompanied him once in a while to church.

When Keith called and asked if he could take Gabe and me out to dinner one night on the upcoming weekend, I told him Gabe would be with his father the night he suggested. I asked him if he would just take me.

He hesitated and then asked, "Well, can I get back to you on that?"

We had a good laugh before he agreed to just take me. His playfulness was a surprise, because although he had a warm demeanor, he seemed a little more serious and reserved than this antic would suggest. I accepted his invitation, or maybe it was Keith who accepted mine.

I enjoyed his company, his sense of humor, his knowledge of the outdoors, his stories about growing up in rural Oklahoma, and the fact that he liked Mexican food as much as I did. He often included my young son in our dates and showed interest in Gabe's sporting events. We spoke very little about our former spouses. A friend of mine, who knew Keith's son, told me that Keith's first wife had died when their daughter went off to college and their son was still in high school. As his children were grown, educated, and on their own when we met, I assumed the loss of his wife was several years prior to our meeting.

In spite of the fact that I was very attracted to Keith and found myself looking forward to his calls and company, I was guarding my heart. However, the more time I spent with him and the more time he spent with Gabe, the more my barriers broke down. When it appeared that this man was becoming an important part of what looked like a bright future, it was time to have him meet the folks.

When Dolores and Trevor met Keith, they welcomed him into the family as if we were already married. There was an instant D&T stamp of approval. Dolores's eyes twinkled as if she had discovered a treasure chest full of gold. I could almost hear her thinking, *Now this is more like it.* She never pushed, preached, or offered advice. Instead, she waited patiently, prayed, and rejoiced when God revealed His plan for Keith and me to wed.

Almost two years after I talked Keith into taking me out to dinner, even without Gabe, we announced our engagement. We first told our children, then Keith's and my other family members, including of course Trevor and Dolores. Finally, we told various friends and the people in the church we attended.

We announced our intentions at a choir practice. A dozen people jumped up smiling, laughing, and shaking hands with us. The woman who directed the hand-bell choir said they would love to play at our wedding ceremony. There was an atmosphere of celebration for the rest of choir practice. But the next Sunday afternoon, it came to my attention that not everyone in the church community felt jubilation at our pending nuptials

After church, Gabe and I were getting ready to go on a bicycle ride with Keith, who had not yet arrived for the outing. One of the ladies from the church called and asked if she could talk to me for a few moments. She was not a close friend to Keith or me. But still, I was delighted to hear from her. I readied myself to be gracious with a thank-you to her well wishes. Instead, the conversation went in an entirely different direction.

"We have just been made aware of Keith's intentions to marry you. Is that correct?" she asked.

"Yes, we are very excited. We hope all of our church family will attend the ceremony," I said.

"How does your little boy feel about it?" she asked. I thought that was a strange question but proceeded to answer her as best I could.

"He likes Keith very much. Honestly, I think he believes he actually is marrying Keith's son and getting a big brother. They seem to have some stuff in common like sports and…"

She cut me off. "There are many things in a marriage besides similar interests. And as you well know, a successful marriage is not always possible."

I couldn't breathe. Her emphasis on the words *you well know* hit a stinging blow. It was no doubt a reference to my divorce.

She didn't give me much time to recover before she continued. "Look, many of us from the church believe that it will be a great match for you. You will have someone to help raise your son. You will certainly be elevated financially. But what about Keith? Have you thought about him? I mean, he is at least ten years older than you. His children are raised, educated, and on their own. Why would he want to start over now with you and your young boy?"

"I—I don't under understand," I stammered as the rock of shame deposited itself in the pit of my gut. She hit all the nerves. I was a single mother and divorced. Keith was older than me and should have been looking forward to living the "empty nest" life and not reworking his world through the lens of rearing another child. I had no idea about the money thing. As far as I knew, Keith was a government worker of modest income making not a great deal more money than I was. He certainly didn't appear to be a rich man. In the middle of my mental stock taking and construction of a defense strategy, my Celtic/Italian temper came roaring through. For my conversation partner, there was no warning of the swift blows about to be delivered by a black belt in tongue.

"Did *you* ever stop to think about Keith?" I asked her.

"What?" she asked.

I repeated the question with intentional slowing in speech and emphasis on each word as if speaking to a small child. "Did *you* ever stop to think about Keith? Have you considered that he loves me, and you are saying hurtful things in an attempt to dissuade the woman he loves from marrying him? How do you think he will feel about *that?*"

"Well, I am not trying to do anything of the sort." She sounded a little more subdued while trying to pick up her end of the conversation.

I decided to let her have both barrels. "Let me clue you in. I don't need anyone or their money. I have made my way since I was thirteen years old. No one has ever handed me anything. My son has a father and doesn't need another one. His dad helps support him and is involved in his life every step of the way. Together, we are privately educating him and seeing to his welfare in all aspects. Keith loves me, and I love him. We will work out whatever hardships may be represented by age difference, previous marital status, children, or interfering do-gooders. Believe me when I tell you that he is going to hear about this today. And it is obvious to me that you do not know him as well as you think, because he is going to be ticked off royally at this antic of yours."

Boom! Done and done. I hung up and called Dolores.

When Trevor answered the phone, he heard my fury and tears. I greeted him and asked to speak to Dolores. He handed her the phone immediately and said, "This does not sound good." Before he let me talk to her, he said, "I love you."

"I told you they would never accept me. I told you so," I informed Dolores through broken sobs.

"Who won't accept you, hon?" she asked. I relayed the words of my recent phone visitor. I left out my responses, however.

She was silent throughout my rant as I poured out my pain. Finally, she said, "Oh my."

I cried into the phone and was grateful Gabe was upstairs trying to see if his action figures could slide all the way down the banister without toppling over.

"Didn't you just tell me that the church members greeted this news the other night with joy?" she asked.

"Yes." I blew my nose.

"I don't think this woman speaks for many within the church community. She is one voice, only one. Whatever her problem, Laura, it is her problem. I feel certain, and so does Trevor, that God has sent you and Keith to each other so you both can have another chance at love after being in first marriages that ended in great pain. And it is my conviction that the majority of your church family agrees with us."

Her words were soft but firm as she talked me off the ledge.

"Really? Do you think they all really do accept me? If that is true, why did she say all these things?" I asked. Fighting your way out of shame demands you become your own personal advocate. But it never hurts to have an ally when you are in the battle.

I could almost hear Dolores smile over the phone. "No, dear, perhaps they don't all accept you. Not everyone in the world, at work, in school, in church, or life in general will always accept any of us. But let's take a step back here. Why do this woman's words carry more weight than the words of congratulations at the choir rehearsal? What is this really all about? You know people can hit us in our most vulnerable places when we least expect it. And you, my dear, have always been worried that you would not be accepted and that you were not good enough.

"Sometimes, I think you seek the approval of the wrong and irrelevant people around you. But the bottom line is simple. Is what she says true?"

"Is what true?" I asked. I was hoping for a little more commiseration and support for my righteous indignation here. It appeared I was looking in the wrong spot. Dolores had a habit of hitting the nail on the honest head and never allowing self-pity to cloud up the landscape of fact and logic.

"The accusations she leveled at you. Is it true that you are looking for a dad for Gabe and that you need someone to bail you out financially? Is any of that true, Laura?" she asked.

"No, of course not. Of course it isn't true." How could she ask such a thing?

"Good answer. And *that* should be the end of *that*, Laura. If you had hesitated for a moment, I would have reminded you that in the last few years I have seen you blossom into a competent single mother, a smart business woman, and capable fiscal steward without help from anyone. We should know. How many times have you declined our attempts to help out with expenses? And remember, my dear, Keith wanted to set the date right away after he proposed. But you refused until all your bills from the divorce are paid off. Somehow, that doesn't fit the picture of the gold digger this woman is accusing you of being.

"There is another thing to consider in these lies that are being leveled against you. If money was your motive, why wouldn't you have gone after one of the rich doctors that work in the same facility as you?

"But let me ask you to, for a moment, forget her words and try to see that she has a hidden agenda here. You don't need to know what it is. But your pain will lessen if you just understand that whatever is going on with her is about her and not you or Keith. You can ask God to give her whatever it is she needs to find her way through this without hurting others. Perhaps, she was a close friend to his late wife. Perhaps, she had someone else in mind for Keith. Perhaps she is protective of him as he has suffered so much. Instead of vilifying her, offer compassion and pray for her," she advised me.

"Right," I whispered.

I didn't think it was a good idea to fill Dolores in on my part of the conversation, in light of her words about compassion.

Dolores continued. "You and Jack divorced. That is what happened. You cannot spend the rest of your life feeling less than others because of it. Instead, you, Jack, and Keith all need to be about helping Gabe adjust and be a happy person. And from what I have seen, Keith is a gentle, patient, and loving person who plans to be part of that process. Am I right about that?"

"Yes, ma'am. You are right about that." Clouds were lifting and tears were stopping. The truth was shining back at me from the lens of unconditional love.

"Now, what are your plans for today, hon?" Dolores asked me while silently announcing that pity-pot time was over.

"Gabe and I are going for a bike ride with Keith," I told her.

"Oh good. Well, you go on that ride and you know that God is blessing all three of you with a second chance at love and family. I don't think this woman is an enemy, but for now you must distance yourself from her and her words. You, my dear, rest in the love of the others in that community who want to see Keith happy and realize that you are what makes him happy, okay? Whatever you do, don't falsely accuse the others in that church, and please don't punish them by taking action that might appear to hold them responsible for this incident.

"Before you go to bed tonight, read Isaiah 43:4. That is all you'll ever need to know." She ended our conversation by offering her blessing on the three of us.

"Okay," I said as Gabe came roaring down the stairs with his action figures held over his head in simulated flight.

"What's wrong, Mommy? Are you crying?" he asked with genuine concern.

"Yes, I was, honey. But Mommy is all okay now," I assured him.

He went outside to engage Augie the pug in a game of action figures versus the alien flat-nosed doggie. I copied the suggested Scripture down immediately and posted it on my refrigerator. It said, "You are precious and I love you" (Isaiah 43:4). She was right. That was all I would ever need to know.

When Keith arrived, I told him what had happened. He snorted and said, "That's a lot of nonsense. If that's how they feel, let's take the family and go to Vegas."

"Vegas? No! I will not be married with plastic flowers, a wedding chapel that looks like a Barbie cutout, and Elvis on every corner. I want to be married here, in this church, with our family, our friends, and our pastor. I love all the people of this church. I want them to be part of our celebration," I insisted.

"Why? You just said..." he started.

I rephrased but repeated what Dolores said. "Because if we don't include our real friends and those we love, we will be excluding them from the joy of our celebration. They deserve to be part of our happiness, especially since so many of them stood with us in our pain and sadness. If we don't share this special time with them, then we are holding all of them responsible for the actions of one person."

Thank you, Lord. I am Dolores's daughter after all, I thought.

"Okay." Keith didn't even pretend to understand. This was probably the first time he saw the truly fierce determination that was part of the new fabric beginning to define this woman he planned to marry. As I looked at him, I could see admiration in his eyes. I liked what I saw. My future husband had no way of knowing that his future wife was rising from her knees to face her lifelong enemies of shame and unworthiness, this time wearing the shining armor of God's love and of his love.

Later, as I tucked Gabe into bed, he looked up and asked, "Mommy, how do you know when you find someone you really want to be with forever? How do you know you found someone to love?"

I silently prayed and asked God to give me the right words to explain this to my little guy. I took a deep breath, kissed him goodnight, and said, "When you look into their eyes and see the person you want to be."

The River of Life

When the stream picks up more water and begins to carve the less parched land, the recipient opens to the nurturing and sustenance provided by the life-giving flow. When the land takes on its own life, although still connected to its life source, it begins to produce fruit and deliver gifts.

CHAPTER 17

Standing in the Pain of Life with Love

Keith and I visited Dolores and Trevor as often as we could, even though separated by over two hundred miles. Whether it was over the phone or in person, Dolores remained my primary spiritual advisor. I knew I could take any questions, doubts, or issues to her.

During one of our visits, I was particularly sad and tearful. When we got some time alone, I confided that a friend of mine recently had lost her baby girl only hours after delivery. I knew it was safe here to talk about the unfairness and to ask how God could allow such things to happen. I didn't know what to do. I pleaded with her to help me find a way to help my friend.

Dolores took my hand and asked me what answer God could give that would satisfy the question and soothe the raw pain my friend was experiencing. I just shook my head and admitted I did not know. She then shared a tragic event from her own life.

Dolores lost her firstborn son five weeks after his birth. I'd had no idea because she'd never mentioned this to me. It was my turn to hold her as she remembered her loss afresh. In the conversation, she taught me a valuable lesson about friendship and ministry in times of tragedy.

She told me there really was not a lot I could do for my friend to make it "better," but there were several things I should not do that could make it worse. As we shared a cup of tea and fresh-baked cookies, Dolores imparted lessons she had learned during her walk through one of her own darkest hours.

Even though her voice shook and was diminished in volume, she told me, "Sweetheart, don't tell her you know how she feels, because you don't. Do not remind her she has other children, and she should concentrate on them. For quite some time, she will have all she can do to concentrate on just putting one foot in front of the other. Refrain from reminding her that she is young and can have more children. No person ever replaces another person."

She paused to drink tea and wipe tears from her eyes before continuing. "Do not hesitate to be by her side when she needs to cry, rant, blame, or pray. There will also be days when she wants to be alone. You must honor that wish, even when you want to be with her.

"There may be times when she blames God and refuses to seek His counsel. People who are offended by her feelings and try to convince her that her loss is God's will are wrong, and they may drive her deeper into the depths of pain and depression.

"Your friend, my dear, will rely upon your patience as she walks these next tedious steps while processing her loss, her faith, and her life. Time will lessen the intensity of her pain on some days, but she will never completely recover from this loss. People who try to hurry her grieving process are attempting to find a way around the pain and sadness they feel. But her true friends will stand with her in the pain, patiently and lovingly, without focusing on how to escape from their own discomfort."

She was silent for a few minutes and then told me, "The most important thing you can do, Laura, is hold her intentionally in prayer every time she comes to mind. And never give up on the God who is holding her gently and tenderly in His loving hands."

I leaned over and kissed Dolores's tear-streaked cheeks. We sat holding hands, praying, crying, and resting in the love of one another and the God who hurts when His children hurt. I drank in the wisdom that she offered through her tears of validity.

That night, as Keith and I were alone in the guest room at the home of my dearest friends, I told him what Dolores had said about helping my girlfriend. He snuggled down, in bed, next to me and said, "Sounds like the wise words of a woman who knows how to be a friend to another woman."

I fell asleep knowing that Dolores absolutely knew how to be a friend. Over the years, she had prayed *for* and *with* me. She held, respected, and stood by me, giving no voice to her own discomfort or inconvenience. Impatience never caused her to distance herself from me, even when realizing there was little she could do to lessen my pain.

That afternoon in her kitchen, Dolores modeled a beautiful gift of aging. She shared wisdom afforded to those who have lived long enough, and experienced enough, to be considered valuable and authentic teachers. As I reflected on our relationship, I realized she had indeed lived that wisdom from the first day our relationship began to evolve. Among other things this woman represented in my life, Dolores answered the call to truly be a friend to me and to teach me how to be a friend to other women.

CHAPTER 18

Times Were Changing

When weather and our schedules permitted, Keith and I traveled to Montrose to see some very special people in our lives, including Trevor and Dolores. How blessed I felt that my husband understood my need to regularly return to the woman that God had sent to fashion me.

In trying to see many people in small time increments, we were rarely on time to any one appointment with friends or family. Dolores was a stickler for punctuality and became annoyed when others were late. Trevor generally made light of the issue by laughing and saying, "In this house, being behind by ten minutes is the same as an hour."

Dolores would furrow her brows, look over the lenses of her wireless eyeglasses, and pretend disapproval as she said, "You know, my dear, you're late." Then I would get the warm smile, hug, and kisses bestowed by the loving parent on the long-awaited child.

As Trevor approached his late eighties, his health began to rapidly deteriorate. We were rarely treated to his easy belly laugh and sense of humor. The couple no longer traveled the world and seldom left Montrose. Dolores showed me, by her tender care of and patience with her husband, what it means to be together in sickness and in health, for better and for worse.

She was vigilant about his diabetic meal requirements, diligent about his medication schedule, and outwardly oblivious to the bouts of ill temper that can often accompany poor health. Every morning, she rose to make a breakfast of turkey bacon and English muffins with peanut butter (Trevor's favorite) and go about her daily routine while humming her unrecognizable tune.

She maintained a sweet countenance and a sense of humor. She never failed to joke when someone sent a card or letter with her name misspelled. She kidded me constantly about arriving late, even when I was on time or early. It became a joke between two people who truly loved one another and needed to infuse comic relief into the relentless uncertainty where Trevor was concerned.

She stayed up late at night to make sure Trevor was safely into sleep before going to her own bed. It was during these late nights, when Trevor and Keith were in bed, that she and I often shared herbal tea and chats. We discussed the latest books we were reading, church politics, raising children, and relying on the Lord to navigate through life. She delighted in my decision to return to school and finish my bachelor's degree when I was fifty years old.

The school schedule and work were tiring, especially since I kept a full-time, home-based business going in addition to taking care of a husband and being as involved in Gabe's life as teenagers permit. My schedule and commitments left little time for the same amount of traveling to the Western Slope as we had previously enjoyed.

With the love and support of Trevor, Dolores, Keith, and several good friends, I started a sacred dance ministry at my church. Dolores and I often discussed finding and using the gifts given to us by God and then using them for His glory. I had come from a long line of dancers and had loved dancing since I was a little girl. Opportunities to dance in worship were limited because of disagreements about what dance could and should be in "religious" settings. There was disapproval from some church members and leaders because they felt this art an inappropriate offering as a gift from and to the Lord.

Over the phone or on the occasions when I was able to see Dolores, she brought me into the reality that God does not give inappropriate gifts. She encouraged me to continue studying and finding ways to worship, praise, and pray through sacred dance. And at the reception of insults and sometimes even threats of people walking out if we danced in worship, Dolores reminded me who I really danced for and why. The other opinions, although hurtful, fell away in light of the majority of congregants who were beginning to love the artful expression of praise, worship, and prayer in the form of movement.

I danced on, pursued my education, and got to Montrose as often as possible. In the fall of 1999, Dolores's husband of sixty-three years, the man who had nicknamed her Rosebud, passed away. It was only a few months after he had celebrated his ninetieth birthday.

We grieved the loss of our friend Trevor, and we worried about Dolores. I had heard it said that when people are together for a lifetime and one dies, the other soon follows. We feared Dolores would not be with us much longer. Our worries were not necessary, however. This lady was a self-defined woman long before it became a popular posture.

Brokenhearted as she was over her loss, Dolores had her own interests and purposes. These sustained her and allowed her a full, productive, and active life even after she found herself a widow. She refused to stop driving, although she was close to ninety years old. She did all of her own shopping, remained in and cared for her home, and, of course, relished entertaining her guests who came from the big city over the hills. She volunteered at her church, lent her voice to church leadership issues, lunched with friends, took care of her roses, made a monthly visit to the Russell Stover Candy Store, and read several books a week. Every day, she took a brisk walk that left many of her companions panting and looking for the nearest bench (including yours truly), and she still made killer chocolate desserts.

She never stopped surprising Keith and me with carefully selected presents sent for birthdays and at Christmas. Her energy and determination inspired me and left me awestruck. She laughed out loud at the advertisements encouraging women in the quest to stop or attempt to reverse the process of aging. She felt the term *anti-aging* was preposterous and that there was only one way to stop aging. Dolores felt she wasn't ready for that quite yet. I knew I certainly wasn't ready for her to stop aging. I saw her as more vibrant, vital, and beautiful with each passing year. I prayed she would be around for a very long time to come.

CHAPTER 19

Dance, Little One, Dance

Next to my husband, Dolores was my biggest supporter when I decided to pursue my master of arts degree. Discovering my gifts in dance and writing was due, in large part, to Dolores telling me it was time to find my gifts and then dedicate them to God, the author of all good gifts. She fully endorsed the concept of periodic personal redefinition.

If the time and effort it took to get the bachelor's degree seemed excessive, they were nothing compared to what it took to get the master's. I had little time to go anywhere but the library, when I wasn't working full-time and trying to manage home and church commitments. Throughout my educational endeavors to obtain the BA and the MA, my reading skills did not improve appreciably. The amount of literature and research I read for the graduate degree was staggering. I often felt overwhelmed and as if my pursuits in higher education were misdirected or mediated by something not strong enough to sustain them. The discouragement I felt at not knowing exactly what discipline to declare sometimes showed through in my conversations with Dolores.

On one visit, we sat on her couch, drinking tea, and talking. She asked me how school was going, and I told her I was at an impasse because I couldn't figure out what God wanted me to do with this education.

She asked, "Well, where do your passions lie? What do you think He has gifted you in?"

Sometimes when Dolores asked a question, I sensed that she probably already had the answer and was just waiting for me to figure things out.

"Dancing and writing," I told her.

"Then there is your answer. Do something that you are already gifted in, and it won't seem so daunting."

The path began to develop with encouragement from Dolores, support from Keith, and guidance from my MA committee. The degree would be in "Storytelling through Creative Movement," with emphasis in sacred dance. Dolores was thrilled with the decision, and as usual, she was right. The journey wasn't so much about more letters after my name. It was about finding where I was to serve the God who had served me.

As my knowledge on the subject of sacred dance increased, I became a more credible resource for the leaders of our church while they considered reintroducing this ancient, sacred art into worship. Although there were still voices of dissent, there were more voices expressing an appreciation for dance as enhancement of the worship experience. The dance team received requests for dance to be done at certain junctures of the liturgical calendar, holy holidays, and in support of sermon topics.

Dolores and I prayed over the direction of my education and my ministry. We asked God to bless this ministry and use it to His glory. There is a saying, "Be careful what you pray for. You just might get it."

And "get it" we did.

Soon our church began to see the dance ministry as one of prayer, praise, and worship. The leaders and parishioners endorsed workshops on the healing power of movement. Requests began to pour in to minister through dance at other churches, workshops, and retreats. Answering the call to share my education and gifts in dance took a toll on my ability to travel to Montrose as much as I wanted.

I apologized to Dolores, on many occasions, for my negligence in visitation. Her response was always the same: "God has gifted, called, educated, and now is sending you. This is what He does, my dear.

Answer the call. He loves you, child. I love you. Now do what you have been born to do. And do it with the love of the one who gives life and gifts so that we may glorify Him here on earth. And don't allow the joy of doing His will to be cramped up with guilt over not being here as often as you used to be, or by bending to those who criticize you, your gifts, or your ministry.

"It is time to dance, little one, dance."

CHAPTER 20

Traveling the Closet

When we were able to get to Montrose, Dolores was my first priority. She was that drink of water I needed to keep me focused in what was becoming a fragmented life of work, study, and home/church obligations as well as building the dance ministry. She delighted in seeing Keith and me no matter how infrequent our visits.

Dolores's patience with me may have grown, even in the face of my chronic tardiness. But her impatience with remaining in this world, as she grew older, also increased. At age ninety-six, Dolores shared with me that when she visited her doctor, she asked if he could please find something wrong that would take her home to her Lord. She said this jokingly as she lifted just one eyebrow, peered at me over her eyeglasses, and tried to look stern. Much to her dissatisfaction, the doctor always replied, "No, Dolores, you are very fit for your age and quite healthy really."

She questioned why God was leaving her here without her life partner, many of her friends, one of her children, and in a body that was so healthy there was no escape for an increasingly restless soul. Because I never thought of her as slowing down, I didn't see Dolores slipping away. But as she neared the last few years of her nineties, things changed for this woman I loved so dearly. It was clear the days were coming to an end when she would tease me for being late, make jokes when her name was misspelled, and gracefully glide around her domain while humming an unknown tune.

When Dolores was ninety-seven, she suffered a fall. Only minor injuries were sustained. However, she accepted the fact that she could no longer live alone. She and her children decided it would be best if she moved into an assisted living center. Because this decision was sudden and unexpected, there wasn't time for Dolores to clean out her house and disperse her belongings. That job fell to her loved ones, including Keith and me.

During the process, Dolores's daughter gave me one of my most prized possessions. It was Trevor's Bible. As I clutched the book in the middle of half-packed boxes, bare walls, and the disorganization that accompanies moving, the wide screen in my mind presented memories. I replayed scenes from many times I had spent in this house with people I had come to see as my parents. Cold reality set in. Trevor was gone, and Dolores was losing her independence. I would never sit in this living room or kitchen again with Dolores, having tea and chatting about things large and small.

Interrupting my private viewing of the past, her daughter offered me a special assignment.

Dolores, like me, loved her clothes. She was trying to decide which items to keep in her new, very limited space. I was asked to help her sort through clothing and arrange her closet. This was a task no one else in the family wanted. When I readily agreed to do this, there was an audible, collective sigh of relief.

At this point, Dolores suffered from macular degeneration and was dependent upon others to be her eyes. She did, however, still possess a keen sense of feel, articulate speech, cleaver wit, sharp memory, and unwavering sense of humor. As we went through her closet, Dolores told me stories about the various pieces I presented to her.

That afternoon, we traveled through the past—just Dolores and I. When I brought her a garment, she ran her hand over it and explained where she had bought it or where Trevor bought it for her. Each piece afforded opportunity for her to share details of their life together.

Like a little girl, she giggled at the memory of spilling French chocolate on a silk blouse and asked if the stain was still there. She took me through Greece and Turkey at the touch of a woolen jacket and shared some of Trevor's comical photographic exploits in that part of the world. A velvet scarf reminded her of the midnight sun in Norway. She lovingly pressed a garment to her cheek that reminded her of their travels in the United Kingdom and asked if I still loved the English lavender she had brought back for me from England.

Her reminiscing brought more than one tear to her eyes, and to mine. We laughed, and cried, as she related the antics of the man she married more than seventy years earlier. These were tears of gratitude. Dolores had no time for, or interest in, ruining good memories with sadness over inevitable and uncontrollable life elements, like the passage of time.

For the better part of four hours, others decided what to do with toasters, gardening supplies, books, and dishes. But Dolores and I cruised, flew, and drove our way through her life. We were in France, Spain, Norway, Greece, Turkey, Denmark, the Holy Land, the United Kingdom, and many places in the United States.

I believe that we humans, especially women, know when we are about to be brought into the corridors of life-altering change. Dolores taught me to never shy away from my inner wisdom. She helped me embrace that sensation and to do or say what needed to be done or said while there was still time.

After we sorted through clothes and returned home from our travels, I took Dolores's frail, thin, and cool hand in mine. I stroked her cheek and told her I loved her more than just about anybody I had ever known. I thanked her for the sacrifices she made in time and energy for me. I wanted her to know she had helped me see and become the person God had created me to be as wife, mother, dancer, writer, storyteller, and mostly, woman of God. I thanked her for suffering with me and helping me address and free myself from the wounds that could have kept me bound in a lifetime of self-pity with destructive choices and behaviors.

She struggled to see me through almost sightless eyes, squeezed my hand, and said, "You are welcome, my dear. I have loved you from the first day I met you. Someday, you will know how much, and it will be your turn to love another woman or women into the kingdom. I need to sleep now."

I helped her to her bed, where she fell asleep after I tucked her in and kissed her forehead. While she rested, I sat in her chair to await my husband's arrival.

When Keith came to get me, he said I looked tired. He asked if the task was tedious and in some ways sad. I thanked him for his concern and assured him I was fine. Truthfully, I was better than fine. I was grateful for the assignment declined by everyone else. I knew the memories of this day would serve to comfort me when the earthly ties between Dolores and me were severed.

As we left the assisted living center, I leaned against my sweet, loving man and confessed, "You know, baby, I think I have jet lag."

To the Ocean

The drop became a stream and turned into a river that nourished the once dry, lifeless land. But ultimately it was required to move into the vast body of water that was always the true, and final, destination.

CHAPTER 21

Mourning into Dancing

Two months before Easter 2011, my pastor asked if the church dance team would minister through movement at Easter services. I said yes and gave him my choice for a worship song. The reason I chose that particular song was because it tells of Christ's promise to deliver us from this troubled, conflicted, and violent world in frightening, war-riddled times. I explained I was not sure when, in my life, I felt more helpless about the future of our planet, our young people, or our country. Pastor agreed that Easter is a time to remember the promise and look with hope toward heaven, regardless of our earthly fears and uncertainties.

The dancers began rehearsal six weeks before Easter. The rehearsal schedule was demanding. The dance was highly energetic and contained complicated choreography. It was challenging, exhilarating, and exhausting. On Sunday, April 24, we danced at all three services to honor the Lord Jesus Christ, remember His promises, and help our parish collectively look to Him for our hope.

Because I was exhausted after such a grueling schedule, Keith took me to a mountain condo, the day after Easter, for some rest. It was there I got the call—Dolores had passed away.

My husband had gone into the nearby town of Silverthorne that morning, and I was alone when the news arrived. I wrapped myself in a woolen blanket, sat out on the porch of our condo, and watched the birds searching for food. I was oblivious to the twenty-degree temperature and blowing snow. I was glad to be alone. I had all I could do to referee the battle between my heart and my head.

My head said, "Dolores was one hundred years old and could no longer see or hear well. Although she did not complain, she often asked what was detaining God and why He was not coming to get her. In her opinion, he had rather fallen behind schedule."

My heart remained silent and just hurt.

My head argued, "You are being selfish. She wanted to go home. You should not be sad. Rejoice for her, and be glad you helped celebrate her one hundredth birthday. Be grateful you knew her and for the wonderful blessing she was in your life."

My heart remained silent and just hurt.

My head can be stubborn. It doesn't like pain and was determined to infuse reason into this discomfort. "Aren't you glad you had that conversation with her? You know the one where you told her how much she meant to you, how you admired her, and how grateful you were to have her in your life. You thanked her for being your mentor and friend. You got the chance to tell her you loved her and, in some ways, to say good-bye. There now, doesn't that make it all better?"

My heart remained silent and just hurt.

My head gave up, and my heart spilled forth tears of human grief that defied logic and rejected attempts to offer comfort. I stared at an empty parking lot as I breathed in frigid air that rolled off snow-covered mountains and glided over the frozen surface of Lake Dillon. My tears were met with snowflakes. I felt like God was softly touching my cheeks and assuring me it was okay to love enough to feel loss.

I needed this silence and solitude so I could clearly hear the music coming from the swaying trees and howling wind. I heard the words to the chorus of the dance my team and I did at Easter. I closed my eyes, saw the dance, and felt an uplifting energy—one gift of true peace. In my little woolen cocoon, I swayed as my heart and head reconciled and danced together. The words to the chorus of the song "Days of Elijah" played over and over in my head.

Behold He comes riding on the clouds,
Shining like the sun at the trumpet call;
Lift your voice, it's the year of jubilee,
And out of Zion's hill salvation comes.

The words offered the hope and promise of the God who never forgets us and longs for the day when we will see His glory and be with Him for eternity. Then I knew. I knew.

That is what it was like for Dolores. She beheld Him coming to take her home. She saw Him shining in His glory, ready to welcome her to a place without bodies that betray and loneliness authored by loss of those we love. God promises to turn our mourning into dancing. He is always there, and He never disappoints.

He went one step farther on that cold, white, wintery morning. He turned my dancing into laughter. He reminded me of the times Dolores had teased me about being late and how she joked, sometimes in annoyance, when her name was misspelled. For a brief breath, He treated me to the smell of chocolate brownies and the aroma of herbal tea. Through tears of a heart saying good-bye, I saw the shining rosebud—the woman who had grown me up in Him.

I laughed out loud as I imagined her entering heaven and carefully explaining to the Lord that she was D-o-l-o-r-e-s, like the river in southern Colorado. And no doubt, she peered over her wireless eyeglasses, furrowed her eyebrows, held her arms open for His embrace, and then lovingly informed Him, "You know, Lord, You're late."

"Laura reflecting on the banks of the Dolores
River, July 2013" Photo by Keith Padgett

Final Author Notes

In 2011, at the age of sixty, with encouragement from many of my lady friends, I launched a blog called Livin' What You're Given (http:// livinwhatyouregiven60.wordpress.com). My first entry encouraged women to embrace their vitality, usefulness, and beauty—no matter what their age—and to defy the incorrect messages sold by the worldwide media. I could think of no better example to show the beauty and vitality of aging than Dolores, my mentor and friend. In the next several posts, I drew from my relationship with this remarkable woman, what she taught me, and how God used her to grow me as a child of God, woman, wife, mother, artist, and scholar.

Today, I have celebrated sixty-two years on earth. I am close to the age when Dolores accepted the call from God to parent and teach a broken young woman plagued by shame, guilt, and a dysfunctional past—living a lifestyle that was totally foreign to her own. Dolores had raised two children, taught hundreds, and was enjoying a well-earned retirement with the man who considered her a flawless and fragrant rosebud. Many people would have run as fast as they could in the other direction. But Dolores said yes to God's call, at age sixty-five, without concern for the time or emotional toll this assignment would take on her planned golden years.

At the completion of my postings about her love, her faith, and who she was in my life, I received many responses from friends and strangers. They told me how blessed they were to know Dolores through the blog postings. I treasure each and every response, but perhaps none more than one sent to me by a dear young woman who is among my closest friends. Lisa Alejandre wrote,

> Thank you, Laura, for sharing this woman's life and your relationship to her with so many. You know, Amiga, you are my Dolores.

There are no words to express what I felt when I read that loving note from Lisa. I put my hands in the air in praise of a God whose grace extends beyond anything I could ask for or imagine. I cried tears of joy and thankfulness for my female friends, of all ages and walks of life, who have learned about Dolores and supported me in my journey to become what she and God wanted me to become. And that day, after receiving Lisa's response, I realized two very important things.

First, I fully understood the statement Dolores had made shortly before her death. "I love you so much. Someday, you will understand how much." I know that love now, because I feel it for Lisa and many of my women friends, mentors, and mentees. They compose a sacred circle of the feminine that I feel part of and trust more deeply with every breath I take.

Second, I recognized and thanked God that it is His good pleasure for Dolores, like the river, to continue flowing. She flows through me to teach, nurture, and mentor the beautiful and vital women God puts in my life. I frequently call on my memories of Dolores to help me embrace the gift of aging, with its wisdom and beauty, as I now enjoy my golden years with the man who considers me his flawless and fragrant rosebud.

About the Author

Laura is an award-winning new author. Her short piece, "Mama's Ring," won second place in a writing contest held by Xulon Press in the summer of 2012. In "Mama's Ring," she tells the story of God's grace in offering her reconciliation with her alcoholic mother, after her mother's death. She has presented this story in the forms of writing, oral storytelling, and dance at various venues around Colorado.

She has been a speaker/presenter at women's retreats, workshops, and dance festivals for over ten years. Her presentations and workshops focus on teaching others how to tell their stories and how to dance in praise, prayer, and worship to the Lord Jesus Christ. Recently she has begun ministering through the arts of storytelling and dance at her church, North Highland Presbyterian, in Denver, where she serves as a deacon. She writes a blog called Livin' What You're Given and offers stories of encouragement, recovery, and inspiration through the lenses of experience, faith, and humor.

Laura earned her Master of Arts degree from Regis University in Denver in May 2009. Her MA is in "Storytelling through Creative Movement." Laura's Master's work produced the book *Moving into the Holy*, an instructional guide that teaches dancers and non-dancers the value of sacred dance as storytelling, praise, prayer and worship. She is a member of Alpha Sigma Nu, the Jesuit Honor Society, and she is former president of the ASN Alumni Club in Denver.

Laura has performed, competed in, and taught Irish step dance. She also has performed and taught Messianic dance, African healing dance, and interpretive liturgical dance. Her students have included all ages from preschoolers to adults. She is a competitive dancer with several gold and silver medals to her credit. She is a member of an adult dance troupe at Destination Dance in Wheat Ridge, Colorado, and is co-president of the Rocky Mountain Sacred Dance Guild. She believes that dance is another way to tell our stories. And she finds inspiration for choreography and her stories by traveling the world, as well as by spending time in the Rocky Mountains, especially on the Western Slope of her home state, Colorado.

She lives in Lakewood, Colorado, with Keith, her husband of twenty years. She has one son (Gabriel), two stepchildren (Laurie and Orin), and three grandchildren (Tom, Katie, and Sophia).